BIG GUNS IN THE ATLANTIC

Germany's battleships and cruisers raid the convoys, 1939–41

ANGUS KONSTAM

OSPREY PUBLISHING
Bloomsbury Publishing Plc
PO Box 883, Oxford, OX1 9PL, UK
29 Earlsfort Terrace, Dublin 2, Ireland
1385 Broadway, 5th Floor, New York, NY 10018, USA
Email: info@ospreypublishing.com
www.ospreypublishing.com

OSPREY is a trademark of Osprey Publishing Ltd

First published in Great Britain in 2021

A catalogue record for this book is available from the British Library.

ISBN: PB 9781472845962; eBook 9781472845979;
ePDF 9781472845986; XML 9781472845993

21 22 23 24 25   10 9 8 7 6 5 4 3 2 1

Cover art and battlescenes by Edouard A. Groult
Maps by www.bounford.com
3D BEV by Alan Gilliland
Index by Alan Rutter
Typeset by PDQ Digital Media Solutions, Bungay, UK
Printed and bound in India by Replika Press Private Ltd.

Photographs
All photos in this book are courtesy of the Stratford Archive.

CONTENTS

INTRODUCTION

At 0445hrs on Friday, 1 September 1939, German troops invaded Poland. For the Polish, outnumbered and out-gunned, courage wasn't enough. Poland's hope was that Britain and France would honour their obligation to support them. However, although Britain and France declared war on Germany two days later, there was little these Allies could do to stem the tide of the Blitzkrieg. This widening conflict was an eventuality the high command of the German Navy – the Kriegsmarine – had planned for. So, within an hour, orders were issued that unleashed this powerful naval force upon the enemy. Effectively, that command marked the start of the Battle of the Atlantic. While the longest-running naval campaign of the war is now primarily seen as a struggle between Germany's U-boat fleet and the Allied convoys, at the time its scope was much wider, for in 1939 the Kriegsmarine's U-boats lacked the numbers to seriously disrupt Britain's key transatlantic supply.

Instead, Grossadmiral (Grand Admiral) Erich Raeder, the Kriegsmarine's Commander-in-Chief, was convinced that only powerful surface warships used as commerce raiders could effectively sever Britain's maritime lifelines. So, from the very onset of war, German surface raiders were sent into the Atlantic Ocean, with orders to sink Allied merchant ships. This stratagem was a risky one. Given Germany's geographical position, the raiders had to pass through Allied patrol lines in the North Sea before reaching their hunting grounds. Then, in order to remain there, these ships had to be resupplied on the high seas. The potential rewards, though, were well worth the effort. These surface ship raids started as soon as war was declared. The armoured cruisers *Deutschland* and *Admiral Graf Spee* were already in the Atlantic, and while the activities of the *Graf Spee* are more widely known, the *Deutschland* had a successful cruise too, and she and her crew lived to tell the tale.

A sortie by the battleships *Gneisenau* and *Scharnhorst* were thwarted by German caution, and then by the Kriegsmarine's involvement in the

The forward main guns of the battleship *Scharnhorst*, pictured while in action off Norway in April 1940. In the North Atlantic, these powerful 28cm (11in.) guns meant she and her sister *Gneisenau* could pretty much eviscerate any convoy and escort they came across.

invasion of Norway. Still, other, lesser warships were able to take their place. Starting in late 1940, a series of successful Atlantic sorties was carried out. Their effectiveness was epitomized that November when the armoured cruiser *Admiral Scheer* fell upon Convoy HX-84, sank her escort, and then picked off five merchant ships. The heavy cruiser *Admiral Hipper* was next, sailing on three cruises in late 1940 and early 1941. Not only did she sink several merchantmen, but she also tied down most of Britain's Home Fleet. These Atlantic raids culminated in Operation *Berlin* – the combined sortie of *Gneisenau* and *Scharnhorst*.

The heavy cruiser *Admiral Hipper*, pictured here, and her sister *Prinz Eugen* carried a main armament of eight 20.3cm (8in.) guns, in four twin turrets. These had a maximum range of 30,000m, or 16.2 nautical miles.

The success of this daring and ambitious operation prompted Raeder to increase the stakes. So, in May 1941 he committed Germany's most modern battleship to a similar venture. Despite spectacular initial success, though, this ended in the loss of the *Bismarck*. As a result, Hitler cancelled Raeder's high-gain but high-risk strategy. While *Bismarck*'s famous voyage overshadowed what came before, during this phase of the war these German surface raiders enjoyed considerable success. This book tells the story of these dramatic sorties into the North Atlantic, and Raeder's policy of using his 'big guns' to force Britain to its knees.

INITIAL STRATEGY

Grossadmiral Raeder's commerce-raiding plans were born out of necessity. A veteran of World War I, Raeder had seen the naval superiority of Britain and her Allies at first hand. So, he understood that in the event of another war, his fleet would be hard-pressed to achieve anything of significance against so powerful an adversary. Besides, with the restrictions imposed on Weimar Germany by the Treaty of Versailles (1919), Germany was incapable of building capital ships worthy of the name. As a result, when he was promoted to Admiral in 1928, and assumed command of the Reichsmarine (State Navy), Raeder began developing his own plans. Fortunately, during the early 1920s he had been involved in producing Germany's official history of the naval war. He made a particular study of commerce raiding

The bows of the battleship *Scharnhorst*, pictured in the spring of 1939 as she returned to her mooring off Kiel after a training cruise. Note the ship's crest at her bow. She was deemed ready for active service shortly before the outbreak of war and left on her first cruise that November.

and became a leading expert on the subject. Inevitably, then, this would become the core of his new strategy for any future war with Britain.

Rebuilding the German Navy

Raeder realized that, unlike the coal-burning cruisers and armed merchantmen of the previous war, more modern commerce raiders would have a greater range, and would no longer be dependent on a network of friendly overseas ports. In fact, if they were supported by tankers and supply ships, and had the capability of refuelling at sea, then they might well be able to conduct extensive cruises, and so would have the potential of disrupting Britain's lifeline convoys. This, though, depended on the navy obtaining suitable ships. To that end, Raeder began supervising plans to build a series of purpose-built commerce raiders. Their intended role had to be disguised, as the Versailles treaty of 1919 prevented the building of armoured warships displacing more than 10,000 tons, which could only be used as coastal defence vessels. There was no real political desire to rebuild the German Navy, but the navy was allowed to replace its ageing warships. Raeder used this to push through the building of a *Panzerschiff* (armoured ship), a vessel which was essentially a custom-built commerce raider.

Grossadmiral (Grand Admiral) Erich Raeder (1876–1960) was born in Hamburg and joined the Imperial Germany Navy in 1894. He served with distinction during World War I and fought at Jutland (1916). After becoming chief of the Germany Navy, he oversaw the fleet's expansion and the building of modern battleships.

Officially, *Panzerschiff* A was built to replace the pre-dreadnought battleship *Preussen*, which had served as a coastal defence vessel and tender until being scrapped in 1931. However, this new ship was purpose-built to roam much farther than Germany's territorial limits. Unusually for the time, she was powered by eight diesel engines, driving a pair of propeller shafts and generating over 53,000 shaft horsepower (shp). These gave the ship a top speed of 26 knots, and a range of up to 18,650 nautical miles at 15 knots. She was no coal-burning *Preussen*, though, having four times the range, much better armour and considerably more firepower. More importantly, the *Preussen* had been obsolete even before the start of World War I. *Panzerschiff* A, soon to be named the *Deutschland*, was a thoroughly modern warship, designed for a new kind of war.

The *Deutschland* was also the first of a class of three armoured cruisers. On the day she entered service – 1 April 1933 – the first of her two sister ships was launched in Wilhelmshaven. By the time she was commissioned in late 1934, a second sister ship, the *Admiral Graf Spee*, was already being fitted out in the same naval dockyard. By January 1936 all three armoured cruisers were in service. The British erroneously dubbed them 'pocket battleships' due to their six battleship-sized 28cm (11in.) guns, mounted in two triple turrets. However, with a belt of only 15cm (6in.) of Krupp steel, these ships were no battleships – merely well-protected cruisers. Even the newly re-branded Kriegsmarine didn't quite know what to do with its new warships, apart

The launch of the *Admiral Graf Spee* in June 1934. She was the third of the Reichsmarine's Deutschland-class *Panzerschiffe* (armoured ships), all of which were primarily designed as commerce raiders rather than the coastal defence ships they ostensibly replaced.

from using them to 'show the flag' and cruise as far as Spain, to demonstrate Hitler's support for Franco's Nationalist rebels. By then, though, Raeder's fleet was about to be boosted by its first proper battleships.

During the early 1930s, it was considered that in any future war, the German Navy might be pitted against either France, Britain or both enemies at the same time. There was no intention to engage in a conventional naval battle against these more powerful adversaries. Instead, the Reichsmarine had to come up with an alternative stratagem, involving either hit-and-run tactics, commerce raiding or simply the deterrence of a 'fleet in being'. This latter notion, first proffered by the late-19th-century naval theorist Alfred Mahan, involved forcing the enemy to tie down a larger number of its own ships, in case your own fleet put to sea. For this, though, Germany needed more powerful warships. So, when the French began building their two Dunkerque-class battleships – their first modern capital ships since before World War I – the German naval high command began drawing up plans for their own capital ships.

The result was the Scharnhorst class. The plans for these two battleships were first drawn up in 1932–33, but these were still being tweaked and altered even after the first of these new ships was laid down in early 1933. The trouble was, at the time, the Reichsmarine had no clear design concept for them, or rather none linked to a coherent naval strategy. For the moment, however, that mattered less than the fact that at last the German Navy would have a pair of modern capital ships in its ranks. Like the armoured cruisers, these were officially built as replacements for older pre-dreadnought warships. They were designated *Panzerschiffe* D and E, but would be considerably larger and more powerful than the three Deutschland-class ships. For a start, while they mounted the same 28cm (11in.) guns, there were now nine of them, in three triple turrets. It was hoped that in the future these guns could be replaced by 38cm (15in.) guns.

The displacement of these ships had kept increasing as the plans developed, but it was clear they would far exceed the 10,000-ton limit imposed by the Treaty of Versailles. By then, Adolf Hitler had become Reichskanzler (Reich Chancellor), and the Nazi leader overcame this problem by publicly abrogating the terms of the treaty. It was a huge risk, but he felt that France and Britain would be unwilling to respond by renewing the war. Instead, his government entered into negotiations with the British, who seemed willing to accept this fait accompli. This, in turn, led to the Anglo-German Naval Agreement of June 1935. By then, the Reichsmarine of the Weimar Republics had been rebranded as the Kriegsmarine (War Navy). Essentially, the treaty showed that the British realized the Versailles Treaty was defunct, and that they wanted some formal agreement that would recognize this, while also curbing Germany's naval ambitions. It limited the new Kriegsmarine to 35 per cent of the Royal Navy's total tonnage, which allowed it to build a balanced battle fleet, albeit one too small to challenge British naval superiority.

Hitler would renege on this treaty in 1939, but in the meantime it allowed Raeder to embark on a dramatic expansion of his fleet. This, of course, allowed the Scharnhorst class to be completed without all of the secrecy and subterfuge which had dominated the previous two years. As a result, their final displacement exceeded 35,500 tons, while the ships were protected by an armoured belt up to 32cm (a little over 12in.) thick. The British would dub these vessels 'battlecruisers', on account of their speed and imagined lightness of armour. In fact, they were fully fledged battleships, albeit with a relatively small calibre of main gun. *Panzerschiff* D was launched as *Scharnhorst* a year after the treaty's signing in June 1936, while *Panzerschiff* E became the *Gneisenau*, and was launched that December. Both ships were in service by the start of 1939.

But this was only the start. The Anglo-German Naval Agreement allowed the Kriegsmarine to draw up plans for further expansion. It also left the navy without any real purpose. In July 1935, Raeder's Chief of Staff officially declared that the agreement made any future war with Britain impossible. From that point, Raeder dropped any reference to Britain as a potential enemy. As a result, the strategic plans drawn up the following May dealt with a potential war against the Soviet Union and France, but not Britain. It was in this light that the building of two new Bismarck-class battleships was approved. Plans for *Panzerschiffe* F and G had first been drawn up in early 1934, and these continued to evolve even after the first of these was laid down in Hamburg in July 1936. In February 1939, *Panzerschiff* F was launched as the *Bismarck*; two months later, her sister ship *Tirpitz* followed her down the slip in Wilhelmshaven.

At the time of her launch, *Bismarck* was arguably the most powerful battleship afloat. With eight 38cm (15in.) guns, her armament was no different from Britain's surviving World War I era battleships. However, these German guns were supported by a thoroughly modern fire control system and first-class optics. The two new battleships also had a top speed of more than 30 knots, which made them considerably faster than their British counterparts, while their armoured belt of 32cm at its thickest point was more extensive than in the Scharnhorst class, which meant these new battleships were even better protected. They had an impressive range of 8,410 nautical miles at 15 knots, which, although slightly less than the Scharnhorst

The German Führer Adolf Hitler (1889–1945), pictured during an inspection of the fleet. He never fully understood naval strategy and was averse to unnecessary risk in naval operations. Consequently, German commence raiders were constrained by orders that emphasized caution rather than boldness.

A Type VIIC U-boat, pictured during a training exercise in the Baltic before the outbreak of war. In September 1939, only 14 oceangoing U-boats like this were available for Atlantic operations. At the time, the Kriegsmarine still felt that attacks on transatlantic convoys were better left to surface ships.

class, was still well suited to conducting cruises in the North Atlantic. These battleships were due to enter service from mid-1940.

Meanwhile, Raeder also commissioned a new class of heavy cruisers. These had been forbidden by the Versailles constraints, but from early 1934, Raeder ordered plans for them to be drawn up anyway. One of his main stipulations was that they would have enough of a range to permit them to operate in the North Atlantic. The first two of these were secretly ordered that October, under the auspices of being a replacement for the obsolete and hulked light cruisers *Berlin* and *Hamburg*. Hitler's abrogation of the Versailles Treaty in March 1935 and the London agreement allowed these cruisers to be built more openly, so permitting more to be ordered. In the end, a total of three of them was built, and were launched in 1937–38 as the *Admiral Hipper*, *Blücher* and *Prinz Eugen*. Two were used as Atlantic raiders – *Blücher* was destined to be sunk during the invasion of Norway in April 1940. Each carried a main armament of eight 20.3cm (8in.) guns.

This was only the starting point for Raeder's planned expansion of the Kriegsmarine. While these new warships were being built, he had plans drawn up for an even more ambitious shipbuilding programme. Between 1935 and 1939, Raeder and his staff tried to work out just what kind of future role the Kriegsmarine might have. These deliberations were still taking place in May 1938, when Hitler summoned Raeder and told him that Britain would now be added to the list of potential adversaries. The shocked naval Commander-in-Chief returned to Kiel, and there he ordered a gifted staff officer, Fregattenkapitän (Commander) Hellmuth Heye, to revise the war plans to include a potential war with Britain. Then he ordered Vizeadmiral (Vice Admiral) Günther Guse, heading the navy's Operations Department, to suggest a way any future naval expansion could accommodate this major change of direction.

On 23 September, the two men presented their findings to Raeder. At the meeting, Guse declared that Heye's plan emphasized that 'We cannot successfully try conclusions with Britain by means of battleships.' This suited Kapitän (Captain) Karl Dönitz, the navy's commander of U-boats. He argued that, as it was impossible to engage Britain's battle fleet, any future war against Britain would centre around commerce-raiding in the North Atlantic. He saw his small fleet of U-boats as the striking force which, if expanded, could bring Britain to her knees. Heye supported this too. As he put it, 'Britain's vulnerability lies in her maritime communications. This postulates that all resources should be applied to mercantile warfare.' He went on to argue for an 'all-out attack, at every point, on Britain's shipping lanes. Owing to Britain's dependence on these, such warfare will produce the best results.'

Raeder agreed with this emphasis on commerce raiding, but not with his subordinates' dismissive attitude towards capital ships. For him, battleships and powerful cruisers were vital tools in any campaign against Britain's sea lanes. This scheme, however, depended on the Kriegsmarine having enough powerful ships and U-boats to carry it out. It also presumed that these commerce raiders – surface ships or U-boats – could break through any cordon of British patrols to reach the hunting grounds in the North Atlantic. Admiral Karl Witzell, Head of the Naval Weapons Department, argued, 'Only the heaviest ships could get the Atlantic striking force through.' Konteradmiral (Rear Admiral) Otto Schniewind, earmarked to the new Admiralty Chief of Staff, argued, 'Our fleet should have a nucleus of capital ships.' At the meeting, both Raeder and Guse agreed with Witzell and Schniewind that for this policy to work, the navy needed powerful capital ships.

In other words, whether they broke out into the Atlantic themselves, or merely escorted lighter forces there, past the British patrols, capital ships formed a vital part of this new commerce-raiding strategy. As Guse put it, 'Whether the ships are actually used to effect the breakout of the anti-mercantile striking force into the Atlantic, or are themselves to operate in strength in that ocean, is a question which need not be decided.' Not everyone agreed. Dönitz insisted that his new breed of ocean-going U-boats could do the job, if only they could be built in sufficient numbers. However, Raeder and his other leading commanders doubted the effectiveness of U-boats, even though their new shipbuilding plans included a dramatic increase in the size of the navy's U-boat arm. With the allocation of funding by the German Führer, Raeder's plans for the phased expansion of the Kriegsmarine could now be shaped to reflect these new strategic aims.

This expansionist scheme was known as 'Plan Z', an abbreviation of *die Zielplanflotte* ('the target plan fleet'). Drawn up by Raeder and his staff in 1938, the plan was finally approved by Hitler in early 1939. At the time of its inception, Hitler assured Raeder that a war between Germany and Britain wouldn't come before 1948. So, this became the end-date of Plan Z. In those nine years, Germany was to build another nine battleships or battlecruisers, four aircraft carriers, 12 armoured cruisers, two heavy cruisers and a large number of smaller warships. In the end, only two new battleships and two heavy cruisers were laid down before the outbreak of war in early September 1939. None of these new ships would be built. Similarly, Germany's first aircraft carrier was launched in late 1938, but would never be commissioned.

The outbreak of war brought Plan Z to a standstill and stymied Raeder's plans for a large, balanced fleet. Instead, he would have to wage a naval war against Britain with the handful of ships at his disposal, or nearing completion. The only real beneficiary in German naval circles was the newly promoted Kommodore (Commodore) Dönitz. Being relatively inexpensive and quick to build, his ocean-going U-boats became the new shipbuilding priority in Germany. So, when war came, Germany had planned for just such an eventuality, but it was a conflict it was otherwise unprepared for, at least

in terms of fleet size and capability. Undaunted, Raeder would do his best to wage a naval campaign with the limited resources at his disposal. This meant he would wage the kind of war he and his staff had begun planning for in 1938, and which he had envisaged long before that. His handful of capital ships and cruisers would be used as commerce raiders, and so would spearhead the Kriegsmarine's attack on Britain's sea lanes.

An Allied convoy gathering in a friendly port. The organization of often as many as 50 merchant ships and tankers was a complex business, but at sea they were usually formed into rows and columns, with each ship a set distance from its neighbour.

Protecting the sea lanes

By contrast, the British strategic position was much more straightforward. Everything centred around merchant shipping. In the late 1930s, British farmers produced only enough domestic food to feed roughly half of the population. This, then, had to be augmented by imported foodstuffs, such as refrigerated or tinned meat, cereal crops and fish. Britain also imported a range of other vital goods, such as crude oil, iron ore and chemicals. There was also a healthy import demand for foreign-built vehicles, clothing and other non-essential goods. Clearly, all of these imports had to reach Britain by sea. At this time, Britain had a merchant fleet of over 4,000 ships, of which roughly 2,500 were at sea at any one time. So, in 1939 Britain's major seaports were bustling centres of maritime commerce, as Canadian and US grain and Argentinian beef filled the warehouses.

Without these imports of foodstuffs, the British people would starve. Without the oil and ore, Britain would be unable to operate, maintain and replace its naval forces, and its mercantile fleet. The British Admiralty was well aware of this, and so the protection of Britain's sea lanes was its greatest priority. The trouble was, this was a global challenge. British imports arrived from every part of the world, although the bulk was shipped from Canada, the United States and Australia. Clearly, the protection of these sprawling sea lanes required considerable naval resources. For much of the inter-war period, the Royal Navy was starved of funding, and so its ageing fleet of cruisers and destroyers had to fulfil this role of trade protection, while also supporting Britain's main battle fleet. It was clear that, if a war came, the Royal Navy would be pushed beyond its limits.

Fortunately, an easing of funding restrictions during the late 1930s saw a gradual improvement in terms of fleet size. Similarly, several nations of the Commonwealth, such as Canada, Australia and New Zealand, expanded their own forces in order to ease this global burden. The British Admiralty also realized that its ability to protect its sea lanes depended on other naval powers – most notably the United States and France. As long as they were able to counter the growing threat from

Japan and Italy, then the over-stretched Royal Navy was just about able to cope. Without them, the Royal Navy could find itself spread too thin to protect the sea lanes.

Fortunately, geography lent a hand. Before the war, the bulk of British imports came from the Americas. These sea lanes were sufficiently far away from either Japan or Italy to make attack unlikely from these powers. Instead, it was Germany that presented the greatest threat. Transatlantic shipping followed well-established routes, whether the ships were heading to Britain from South America, the West Indies or Canada. Most merchant ships tended to follow the course of the Gulf Stream, and so the busiest transatlantic route lay between Newfoundland and Ireland. Similarly, shipping coming from the Mediterranean and the Cape of Good Hope also plied well-established sea lanes. Most of these ships converged on the bottleneck of the Western Approaches – the western and south-western approaches to the British Isles. This meant that any German U-boats were likely to concentrate there.

As a result, the Admiralty would concentrate its anti-submarine efforts in this area. Similarly, the implementation of a convoy system worked well during World War I, as it allowed the Royal Navy to make the best possible use of its escort vessels. It had high hopes that inter-war developments in submarine detection – ASDIC or sonar – meant that its escorts had the technological edge over its potential German foes. With new destroyers entering service during the late 1930s, the Admiralty felt reasonably confident that this German threat could be contained. What the Admiralty didn't plan for, however, was the expansion of the Kriegsmarine's ocean-going U-boat fleet after the start of the war, and its new tactics of hunting in wolfpacks. This, combined with the Germans' ability to use French Atlantic ports after the summer of 1940, meant that Dönitz' U-boats became a markedly greater threat than the British had anticipated.

The British battlecruiser *Hood*, pictured lying in Scapa Flow shortly before the outbreak of war. On the left of the photo is the battlecruiser *Renown*. As the wartime base of the Home Fleet, Scapa Flow was ideally placed to help prevent German access into the North Atlantic.

Vice Admiral Somerville's Force H at sea, during early 1941. In the foreground is Somerville's flagship, the battlecruiser *Renown*, accompanied by the aircraft carrier *Ark Royal* and the light cruiser *Sheffield*. In February 1941, this powerful mixed force came close to intercepting *Gneisenau* and *Scharnhorst* as they were heading towards Brest.

The Admiralty's plans to counter German surface raiders also had its roots in the previous war. During World War I, the British imposed a blockade of Germany and sought to contain German naval forces in the North Sea. From its wartime base in Scapa Flow in Orkney, the fleet was able to counter any German sortie, while also supporting the lighter blockading forces, strung out across the top of the North Sea, from Orkney and Shetland to the Norwegian coast. In any future war, the Royal Navy planned to follow a similar course, and the Home Fleet would return to Scapa Flow. In 1939 it was considerably more powerful than the Kriegsmarine, and so in theory should have been able to prevent German raiders from reaching the Atlantic. Despite this, with radar in its infancy, and the North Sea and Norwegian Sea beyond it prone to unfavourable weather, there was always a risk a commerce raider could slip through the British net.

This problem increased dramatically in 1940, following the successful German invasion of Norway. As a result, the British patrol line had to be moved back to the much larger arc stretching from Greenland to Scotland, by way of Iceland and the Faeroes. All four passages into the North Atlantic had to be guarded, and British ships now had to travel farther and remain on station for longer. Although Iceland could now be used as a refuelling base, the business of preventing German access to the Atlantic was now much harder. The Kriegsmarine benefited in other ways too. Now, its surface raiders could travel northwards along the Norwegian coast, protected by an air umbrella. Then, they could pick their moment to make their break-out attempt. The same Norwegian haven was also there for raiders returning home. This, together with the use of French ports, did more to undercut British naval strategy than anything else during this period.

So, in effect, while the Germans were beginning to embrace a new strategy based on long-range commerce raiding, the British were still stuck in the stratagems of the previous war. If for some reason the Home Fleet was unable to prevent the German raiders from reaching the Atlantic, then the British problems increased dramatically. Wartime convoys would only be protected by anti-submarine escorts, which would be unable to guard them against larger surface raiders. The Home Fleet would have to try to hunt down the raiders in the vastness of the Atlantic, while other naval forces such as Force H based in Gibraltar might also be called in to help. So, any successful German sortie would by necessity tie down a disproportionately large number of British warships. It might also lead to the temporary disruption of convoy sailings. All this without the Germans having to fire a shot.

PLANNING FOR WAR

By 1938, the long-term prospects for peace were dwindling. So, both in Britain and Germany, plans were drawn up for a future war between the two countries. In Kiel though, Raeder and his staff continued to believe Hitler when he said that war against Britain was inconceivable. The plans drawn up by Fregattenkapitän Heye were really designed to be initiated during the 1940s, when the Kriegsmarine was powerful enough to challenge British naval superiority. In the meantime, it would be held in readiness as a form of insurance, in the seemingly unlikely event that Britain and France were willing to go to war with Germany as a result of their pledge of support to Poland. As for the Admiralty in London, the political appeasement of 1938 bought the Royal Navy a little more time to build up its strength after decades of underfunding. New ships were being built, including five new battleships, but the first of these would only enter service in late 1940. In the meantime, the fleet would have to use the limited resources it already had.

Grossadmiral Raeder (centre), flanked by two staff officers during a briefing in his Berlin headquarters on Tirpitzufer (now Reichpietschufer). The officer on Raeder's right is his extremely able adjutant, Kapitän-zur-See Erich Schulte-Mönting.

The Kriegsmarine

Raeder and his staff had a few challenges to overcome to turn their commerce-raiding vision into reality. The first of these was how to keep their Atlantic raiders at sea. The *Panzerschiffe* had a respectable range of more than 18,000 nautical miles. This allowed them to range as far as the South Atlantic without refuelling. It was roughly 2,000 miles to the main transatlantic sea lanes, and another 500 miles to the Western Approaches. While the range allowed these ships to remain at sea for months, they

Vizeadmiral (Vice Admiral) Karl Dönitz commanded the Kriegsmarine's U-boat arm during the war, until January 1943, when he replaced Raeder as the navy's Commander-in-Chief. Before the war he tried unsuccessfully to challenge Raeder's emphasis on surface warships as commerce raiders, rather than U-boats, which Dönitz felt were better suited to the role.

would eventually reach their limit in terms of food, ammunition, water and provisions. There was also the problem of potential mechanical failure. So, to keep these ships in the hunting grounds, the Kriegsmarine needed to find a way to replenish them at sea. Raeder's solution was to deploy supply ships in the Atlantic before the raiders even left port.

These ships would carry stocks of fuel, food, water and ammunition, which would operate in concert with his new generation of raiders. While the techniques for refuelling at sea were still in their infancy, German naval observers had been keeping abreast of the latest developments. 'Underway Replenishment' had first been pioneered by the US Navy during World War I, as a means of allowing smaller destroyers to keep pace with capital ships. By 1939, both the US Navy and the Royal Navy had developed the ability to refuel larger warships while at sea, but it was the Germans who got there first, having perfected the technique by the mid-1930s. By 1938, the crews of the *Panzerschiffe* were practising Replenishment at Sea (RAS) operations, working in concert with specially designed *Trosschiffe* (supply ships). While this replenishment was usually carried out when both ships were stationary, the Kriegsmarine was also developing the ability to refuel ships while both vessels were still under way.

The problems of keeping Atlantic raiders refuelled became even more acute with other German warships. Unlike the Deutschland class, which were purpose built as long-range commerce raiders, the new heavy cruisers of the Admiral Hipper class were sleek fuel-guzzling greyhounds, designed for speed rather than endurance. Their range was limited to 6,500 nautical miles at 17 knots. The more commodious two battleships of the Scharnhorst class had a slightly better range of 9,020 miles at 17 knots. With a fuel oil capacity of just over 3,000 and 5,300 tons respectively, this meant that the stationing of supply ships became imperative if these ships were to achieve much in the Atlantic. So, the Kriegsmarine developed its own solution – the Dithmarschen class of *Trosschiffe*. These ships could carry 12,000 tons of fuel oil or diesel – enough to replenish the *Deutschland* or *Hipper* four times over – and carry the ammunition and provisions they needed to stay at sea for months.

Three of them were in service by the time the war broke out, while a fourth would join them in September 1940. In addition, a number of German-flagged tankers or merchant ships were pressed into service to fulfil the same role, albeit without the facilities of these custom-built *Trosschiffe*. The intention was, shortly before an Atlantic sortie took place, several of these support vessels would put to sea and evade British patrols to reach the Atlantic. Once there, they would keep well away from known shipping lanes. Instead, they would loiter in pre-arranged stations, such as off the southern tip of Greenland, the Arctic Sea or the Labrador Sea. If a German raider needed to be resupplied, a rendezvous would be arranged at a pre-determined location. This way, Germany's Atlantic raiders were able to pose a much greater threat than if they operated on their own.

In July 1939, the *Kriegsmarine*'s Operations Division produced a set of guidelines called 'The Atlantic Trade Warfare Plan'. Effectively, this was the rule book for commerce raiders. It argued that these ships had three missions: to sink or capture ships, to disrupt enemy shipping, and to divert the enemy's naval resources into chasing the raiders. While it didn't go into a lot of detail, as at the time Germany wasn't at war with Britain or France, it did impose restrictions. Only Hitler could decide on the level of freedom these commerce raiders enjoyed. In effect, he would decide whether they would be unleashed in the pursuit of 'total war', with little in the way of humanitarian restrictions, or whether they would operate a more humanitarian approach, in keeping with international law. In that case, international prize regulations would govern the way 'prize ships' were stopped, and would ensure that their crews were allowed time to abandon ship before their vessels were sunk.

This plan also stressed the need to avoid battle wherever possible, stating, 'Combat action, even against inferior naval forces was not an aim in itself, and is therefore not to be sought.' Given the size of the Kriegsmarine, it was vital that unnecessary risks should be avoided. Better to avoid action than to risk damage to the raider. The plan also outlined the tactics a raider should use, such as making 'surprise appearances, followed by immediate withdrawal into the ocean wastes, and constant shifting of areas of activity'.

This passage displays Raeder's hand. Having studied commerce raiding in the last war, he knew how to get the best results from his ships in any new conflict. He realized that it was possible that a victim would be able to send off a radio message before she was sunk, and with the numerical superiority of the enemy, it was likely that they could dispatch warships to the area very rapidly. So, it made sense to move to another hunting ground.

Although it wasn't directly included in the plan, Raeder had also given some thought to the best hunting grounds for his surface raiders, as well as the places they could go to lie low while the enemy combed the ocean looking for them. It was important to keep away from known enemy naval bases, such as Scapa Flow, Portsmouth,

The breakthrough that allowed German surface warships to act effectively as commerce raiders came in the late 1930s, when the Kriegsmarine developed a technique for refueling at sea. Unlike modern refueling operations, this was done with the tanker stationed ahead of the warships, with her hoses passed astern of her, like a tow rope.

A U-boat on patrol in the North Atlantic. During the Kriegsmarine's surface sorties into the Atlantic, boats like this served as additional 'eyes and ears' of the raiders, passing on sighting reports to Dönitz, which were then relayed to the raider captains or fleet commanders.

Gibraltar, Halifax in Nova Scotia and Sierra Leone in West Africa. That would reduce the risk of surprise encounters with enemy warships. This didn't always mean concentrating on the busiest sea lanes where enemy convoys would most likely be encountered. Certainly, these main shipping lanes in the North Atlantic between Newfoundland or Gibraltar and the Western Approaches would be lucrative hunting grounds. However, they were also likely to be well protected. For some lighter raiders, better results might be had in the South Atlantic, particularly off the West African coast, or even farther afield, in the Indian Ocean.

Raeder also realized that, compared with German commerce raiders of World War I, his new generation of well-armed raiders had a number of major advantages. First, there was *B-Dienst*. Each ship would carry a team of analysts, translators and cryptographers from the *Funkbeobachtungsdienst* ('Naval Radio Monitoring Service'), usually abbreviated to *B-Dienst*. There to monitor enemy radio signals, the team used sophisticated frequency scanners and direction-finding equipment to find out where enemy convoys were, and to warn the raider of enemy warship movements. This was backed up by a similar service provided from bases in Germany, and later in Norway, Denmark and France as well.

This time, German ships had a new secret weapon. In 1936 the prototype Seetakt surface search radar was introduced into naval service, when it was installed in the *Graf Spee*. In theory it could detect surface contacts up to 10 nautical miles away, but it had teething problems. A better set, the FuMo22, was introduced in 1939, with a surface search range of up to 13 nautical miles. It was fitted in all three of the Deutschland-class *Panzerschiffe*, as well as the two battleships of the Scharnhorst class and the *Admiral Hipper*. While British warships generally had better radar sets, these at least gave the raiders an edge during their attacks on convoys, particularly at night. In theory, these sets had a limited fire control capability, but this wasn't as reliable as the ships' more traditional optical rangefinders. From 1940, *Admiral Scheer* and *Deutschland* (renamed *Lützow* on 15 December 1939) were fitted with the FuMo26 set, which had improved fire control abilities and a range of 17 miles.

Another modern search tool was the Arado Ar 196 floatplane. Each of these raiders carried at least two of these, launched from a catapult. With a range of up to 580 nautical miles, these small aircraft could be used to search for convoys and approaching warships. They could also be used to help direct the raider's guns onto their target. This was an incredibly useful tool for the German raiders, and their captains would make good use of these floatplanes to extend their search radius far beyond the horizon. Another modern development was the Kriegsmarine's deployment of reliable ocean-going U-boats into the North Atlantic. These sent regular sighting reports back to Germany, which could then be passed on to the raiders. Effectively, they acted as additional eyes for the raider commanders. Following the German conquest of France and Norway, the Luftwaffe also began conducting long-range maritime patrols. While inter-service rivalry meant sighting reports were rarely timely, in theory these patrols helped the Kriegsmarine build a better intelligence picture of enemy ship movements in the Western Approaches, the Bay of Biscay and the Norwegian Sea.

Armed with these modern advantages, the raiders would be more effective than their World War I predecessors. Their speed, long range and powerful armament would all make them powerful weapons in the Kriegsmarine's arsenal. This would all go a long way towards making up for their lack of numbers. What Grossadmiral Raeder had to do now was to make sure they could reach their Atlantic hunting grounds and deploy where they could cause the most damage. The problem, even after the fall of France and Norway, was in the raiders managing to slip past the British patrol lines to reach the vastness of the ocean that lay beyond. This, however, was a problem that couldn't be overcome by anything other than careful timing, good judgement, skilful use of the prevailing weather and sea conditions, the latest intelligence and a healthy dose of luck.

The Royal Navy

By 1939 the British were well aware that Germany's *Panzerschiffe* were designed to operate as commerce raiders in time of war. While some dubbed them 'pocket battleships', most of the wiser heads in the Admiralty knew that these ships weren't intended to fight enemy surface ships, unless they had to. Naval intelligence sources had already revealed the impressive range of their diesel engines, while their speed and performance made them the equal of most of the more modern ships in the British fleet. However, the British were also aware that the impressive armament and propulsion systems of the three *Panzerschiffe* had come at a price. Their Achilles heel was their relatively light armour. If only they could be caught by British capital ships or even a squadron of cruisers, then they could be destroyed.

The two Scharnhorst-class battleships were another matter. They were fast and well armed, but they were also well protected. With a top speed greater than

An Allied transatlantic convoy, photographed from a patrolling aircraft from RAF Coastal Command. It is arrayed in four rows and several columns. A convoy would therefore form a huge rectangle of ships, spread out over several miles of ocean.

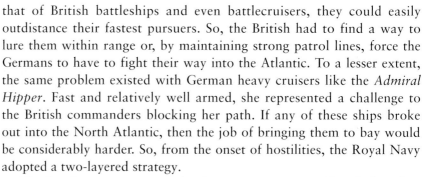

that of British battleships and even battlecruisers, they could easily outdistance their fastest pursuers. So, the British had to find a way to lure them within range or, by maintaining strong patrol lines, force the Germans to have to fight their way into the Atlantic. To a lesser extent, the same problem existed with German heavy cruisers like the *Admiral Hipper*. Fast and relatively well armed, she represented a challenge to the British commanders blocking her path. If any of these ships broke out into the North Atlantic, then the job of bringing them to bay would be considerably harder. So, from the onset of hostilities, the Royal Navy adopted a two-layered strategy.

The first layer was to stop the German commerce raiders before they left the North Sea. This was exactly the strategy which had worked so well in World War I, and the mechanism was already in place to reconstitute it for a new war with Germany. A patrol line – the Northern Patrol – would be established between the North of Scotland and the Norwegian coast near Stavanger. The 'Northern Passage' between these two points

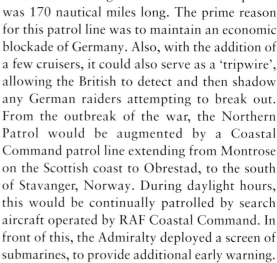

was 170 nautical miles long. The prime reason for this patrol line was to maintain an economic blockade of Germany. Also, with the addition of a few cruisers, it could also serve as a 'tripwire', allowing the British to detect and then shadow any German raiders attempting to break out. From the outbreak of the war, the Northern Patrol would be augmented by a Coastal Command patrol line extending from Montrose on the Scottish coast to Obrestad, to the south of Stavanger, Norway. During daylight hours, this would be continually patrolled by search aircraft operated by RAF Coastal Command. In front of this, the Admiralty deployed a screen of submarines, to provide additional early warning.

If a German sortie were detected, then more powerful units of the Home Fleet could sortie from Scapa Flow and set a course to intercept it. The strength of the Home Fleet fluctuated all the time, but for the most part it was more powerful in terms of capital ships and cruisers than the entire Kriegsmarine. So, at least in theory, its Commander-in-Chief, Admiral Sir Charles Forbes, who flew his flag in the battleship *Rodney*, would have the muscle to stop any German incursion. Another useful tool was intelligence gathering. As well as any intelligence gathered through espionage, the British flew regular reconnaissance sorties over German ports such as Wilhelmshaven and Kiel, to detect any German force movements. This

As the commander of the Home Fleet, Admiral Sir Charles Forbes (1880–1960) was given the task of preventing German raiders from breaking out into the North Atlantic, or of hunting them down if they managed to evade his patrols. He held the post until December 1940.

was supported by friendly coast-watchers in the neutral Scandinavian countries, by another submarine patrol line in the Skagerrak, and by a network of radio intercept stations and direction finders.

If intelligence reports suggested the Germans had put to sea, then the Home Fleet would make a sweep too. In most cases this involved patrolling the line between Orkney and Shetland, and then Shetland and the Faeroes, and across the Norwegian sea around the latitude of Bergen. The danger here was that if a sweep were carried out too early, then the bulk of the Home Fleet would have to return to Scapa Flow to refuel. This would allow the German raiders to slip out while the exits were left unguarded. So, for Admiral Forbes, timing and a thoughtful deployment of force were key. The second line of defence was to extend these sweeps to include all of the choke points leading into the North Atlantic, extending in a thousand-mile arc from the north of Scotland to the eastern coast of Greenland.

Essentially there were five of these choke points: between Greenland and Iceland, Iceland and the Faeroes, the Faeroes and Shetland, Shetland and Orkney, and finally Orkney and the Scottish mainland. The last two were heavily patrolled, and their proximity to Scapa Flow and RAF airfields in Orkney, Shetland and Caithness made it unlikely the Germans would

The Enigma machine was a mechanical encryption device developed by the Germans to protect their military, naval and diplomatic signals. By capturing a machine and breaking its codes, the Allies were able to decipher a number of vital signals sent between the Kriegsmarine's shore bases and its Atlantic raiders.

risk attempting to break out that way. In fact, any attempted German transit of the Pentland Firth to the south of Orkney would be suicidal. The 43-nautical-mile-wide Fair Isle passage to the north of Orkney was little better. Next was the 170-nautical-mile gap between Shetland and the Faeroes. It was patrolled by aircraft based in Sumburgh in Shetland, but it still remained a viable outlet into the Atlantic. Nevertheless, it was still relatively close to Scapa Flow, and so would present more of a risk to a German commander than the two remaining routes to the north.

The first of these, the 240-nautical-mile passage between Iceland and the Faeroes, was closer to Germany than the final one, but it was known to be well patrolled, and British warships were able to refuel easily in Icelandic ports. The final choke point was the Denmark Strait between Greenland and Iceland. It was probably better for the raiders due to its distance from the Home Fleet's base, and for the frequency with which mist banks or sleet and snow reduced visibility there. However, for much of the year pack ice off Greenland reduced the width of the channel, making it easier for the British to cover it with a small screen of cruisers. So, having reached the northern edge of the North Sea, the commander of a German commerce raider had to work his way through the Northern Passage, with its screens of patrol ships, submarines and aircraft. This meant timing the transit so it took place at night. If they passed this line, then they still had to make their way through one of the choke-point channels.

If the Home Fleet failed to detect and stop a raider at any of these points, then it was presented with a much greater problem. The German raider would be loose in the vastness of the Atlantic Ocean, where detecting it was exponentially harder. The British solution was to form hunting groups of warships, which would try to intercept the raider on the high seas. If possible, the escorts accompanying convoys would also be strengthened, and if the German threat warranted it, then some of the older British battleships would be used to help protect the convoys. RAF Coastal Command would stage sweeps over the Atlantic, concentrating on the Western Approaches; farther south, additional aircraft and hunting groups could be called in from other naval stations, such as Gibraltar, Dakar, Freetown or Cape Town. With luck and good intelligence work, the raider could be brought to bay.

The trouble for the British was that the German raider held the initiative, and so the British had to devote a disproportionately large force to counter its actions. This, of course, was one of Raeder's objectives – to divert the enemy's naval resources. The Royal Navy didn't have sufficient resources to protect everything. With commitments in the Mediterranean, Indian Ocean and Far East as well as in Home Waters, there were rarely enough cruisers and capital ships available. Instead, the Admiralty was forced to prioritize its resources, with the bulk of the fleet retained in Home Waters and the Mediterranean. The Royal Navy was overstretched, and the Kriegsmarine knew it. This was particularly true after France was knocked out of the war in mid-1940. Until then, the French Navy could offer some help; after that, the Royal Navy was on its own.

All this was laid down in detail in the Admiralty War Memorandum – a set of war plans that would be put into effect as soon as war was declared. Still, it took time to implement these plans and to organize convoys. Then, as the war progressed, the Admiralty had other distractions. Ship losses were heavy during the first year of the war, while the surrender of France and the entry of Italy into the war dramatically tipped the strategic balance. So too did the fall of Norway, as it forced the British to withdraw the Northern Patrol and cede Norwegian waters to the Germans. All of these developments meant that the Admiralty had far fewer warships than it needed, and so hunting groups became an unaffordable luxury, except in exceptional cases. Instead, it had to protect what it could and concentrate its efforts on 'focal points' where convoy routes converged. In other words, once a raider broke out into the Atlantic, the British had fewer strategic options. With over 40 million square miles of ocean to hide in, the raider held all the best cards.

THE ATLANTIC SORTIES

Grossadmiral Raeder had taken Hitler at his word. He knew that Hitler was planning to invade Poland, and that both Britain and France had pledged to support the Poles in the event of war. However, Hitler assured him that there was little chance that either of these two powers would actually declare war on Germany. As late as the end of August, when the German Army was mobilizing along the Polish border, Raeder was happy to deploy many of his naval resources in the Baltic to support the German invasion. As Konteradmiral Otto Fricke, the Kriegsmarine's Chief of Operations, put it, it was hardly conceivable that Britain would enter the war. Raeder agreed. Surprisingly, when the Polish invasion began on 1 September, both the British and the French sent Hitler an ultimatum: stop the invasion or face the consequences. On 3 September, when this plea was ignored, first Britain and then France declared war on Germany.

For Raeder it was a stunning blow. On hearing the news, he locked himself away with his staff aide, Kapitän-zur-See Erich Schulte-Mönting. With his Plan Z in shreds and his small fleet locked in a conflict Hitler had promised wouldn't come for at least five years, he now had to lead the Kriegsmarine into a war for which it was ill prepared. That said, at least he had taken the precaution of initiating the opening moves of the Kriegsmarine's own war plans, just in case the diplomatic situation deteriorated.

The engine room of the battleship *Gneisenau*. With its powerful Germania turbines powered by steam from Wagner boilers, these engines provided over 165,000shp – enough to power these large battleships at speeds of up to 32 knots. This was significantly faster than any Royal Naval battleship.

This seems like a contradiction – not expecting war yet preparing for it – but it was a sensible operational precaution. Before the invasion of Poland, just in case Britain and France might honour their pledge, a handful of Kriegsmarine surface ships and U-boats had put to sea, in case they were needed. Now, on 3 September 1939, their moment had come.

Opening moves

The Kriegsmarine had already made its move, long before the German tanks rolled over the Polish border. On Monday 21 August, the armoured cruiser *Graf Spee* slipped out of Wilhelmshaven, and two days later she made her way through the Northern Passage without being detected. On 24 August she reached the North Atlantic, after transiting the Faeroes gap. That same day, and late off the mark, the Admiralty ordered the Home Fleet to take up its war station in Scapa Flow. On the day the *Graf Spee* reached the Atlantic, a second armoured cruiser, the *Deutschland*, also left Wilhelmshaven and followed her sister ship through the Northern Passage. She then headed northwards towards the Denmark Strait. Neither ship was detected. At the same time, 16 ocean-going U-boats had also put to sea and were on their way to their patrol areas in the Western Approaches. Other coastal U-boats did the same off Britain's North Sea coast. This, of course, was a precautionary measure, in the event Britain would declare war on Germany.

Two supply ships had preceded the surface raiders into the North Atlantic, and now these ships, the *Altmark* and the *Westerwald*, were in their assigned positions. *Altmark* was waiting for *Graf Spee* 600 miles to the south-west of the Canary Islands, while *Westerwald*, supporting the *Deutschland*, took up her station off the southern tip of Greenland. This reflected the hunting areas for the two cruisers. *Graf Spee* was bound for the South Atlantic, as she was hunting the waters between southern Africa and South America, while *Deutschland* would prey on the transatlantic shipping lanes spanning the North Atlantic. By 1 September, when the *Graf Spee* rendezvoused with the *Altmark* in mid-ocean, she had already passed the latitude of the Canaries. She topped up her fuel tanks again on 3 September, 600 miles to the west of the Cape Verde Islands. That meant that by the time Britain declared war on Germany, she had already reached her South Atlantic hunting ground.

The cruise of the *Graf Spee* is already well known (see Osprey's Campaign 171: *River Plate 1939*). Also, as her area of operations was in the South Atlantic and Indian Ocean, her activities lay outside the geographical boundaries of the North Atlantic, the region we concentrate on here. Less well known, though, is the cruise of the *Deutschland*. Her commander, Kapitän August Thiele, had made better speed than the *Graf Spee* and was reaching the eastern approaches to the Faeroes gap by dawn on 24 August. He knew that Kapitän Langsdorff in the *Graf Spee* was only about 300 nautical miles ahead of him, at the western end of the choke point. So, in case Langsdorff was detected, Thiele decided to continue past Iceland, then curve round to enter the North Atlantic through the Denmark Strait. He reached the north-eastern end of the strait just before dawn on 28 August

and slipped through undetected, screened in part by rolling banks of fog. By late afternoon *Deutschland* had reached the North Atlantic without being detected.

After that, all Thiele and his men could do was to wait. Their supply and waiting area was centred on Cape Farewell ('Kap Farvel' in Danish), the southernmost tip of Greenland. It was here that the *Westerwald* was waiting for them, allowing the *Deutschland* to replenish her diesel tanks. Their allocated supply area was far from any shipping lanes, extending for 150 nautical miles up either side of Greenland and 50 miles out to sea. Thiele, though, elected to loiter 60–100 miles to the south-east of Cape Farewell, within easy striking range of the sea route between Nova Scotia and Britain. The *Deutschland* was still there when war was declared on 3 September, but like Langsdorff in the *Graf Spee*, Thiele was forbidden to begin commerce raiding until he received the appropriate orders. These could only come from the German Führer, and Hitler still believed he could negotiate peace with Britain and France. So, the days turned into weeks, but the order never came.

At first, Thiele took the *Deutschland* off towards the south-east, hoping to be in a better position when his ship was activated. Then, on 5 September, when the *Seekriegsleitung* ('Naval Warfare Command', or SKL) told him there would be no imminent change to his orders, Thiele retraced his course, heading back towards the coast of Greenland. The waiting continued, with the cruiser remaining just out of sight of land, to the east of Cape Farewell. Finally, on Tuesday 26 September, after more than three weeks of war, the communications room on the *Deutschland* received the long-awaited order. Even this was limited, as attacks were only permitted against British merchant shipping. Attacks also had to be carried out within the bounds of international law. At last, *Deutschland* was allowed to begin her cruise. After a final top-up from the *Westerwald*, Thiele headed south.

Thiele reckoned that, by now, shipping on the main Halifax to Britain route was already formed up into well-protected convoys. Well aware that his orders emphasized avoiding a fight with enemy warships, he decided

Under Kapitän Hans Langsdorff, the armoured cruiser *Graf Spee* conducted a wide-ranging commerce raid into the South Atlantic and Indian Ocean during late 1939, but on 13 December she was brought to battle off the River Plate by a force of British cruisers. This shows her just after the battle, in the outer harbour of Montevideo in Uruguay.

The first of her kind, the *Panzerschiff Deutschland* was built to conform to the restrictions of the Treaty of Versailles, which only permitted the Reichsmarine to build warships displacing up to 10,000 tons. While the British dubbed her a 'pocket battleship', she was primarily designed as a commerce raider.

instead to intercept the secondary sea lane between Bermuda and the Azores. Here, he thought, convoys might not have been formed yet, and there was every chance of encountering solitary merchant ships. His hunch was correct. On the morning of Thursday, 5 October he came across the lone freighter SS *Stonegate*, some 600 miles east of Bermuda. The freighter heaved to when challenged, but despite Thiele's orders she sent off a radio distress message, saying she was under attack from a German raider. The *Deutschland* fired warning shots which ended the transmission, but by then it was too late. After allowing her crew to abandon ship, the *Deutschland*'s guns sent the 5,400-ton freighter to the bottom.

B-Dienst intercepts told Thiele that the British had heard the distress signal. The battleships *Revenge* and *Resolution* were in the area, and they and other warships would soon converge on the spot. So, Thiele sped away to the north, hoping to find fresh prey to the east of Nova Scotia. He reached this new operational area on 9 October. He planned to lurk there for a week, just to the south of the main convoy route. At this time, the British dispersed their westbound convoys a little to the east of Newfoundland, allowing the merchant ships to head for their own destination ports in Canada or the United States. Thiele hoped the *Deutschland* would come across some of these solitary merchant ships.

Sure enough, on 9 October she came across the SS *City of Flint*, a US-flagged freighter of 4,963 tons. However, rather than heading for home, she was on her way to Britain, with a cargo of tractors, fruit and grain. Thiele deemed this to be contraband and captured the merchantman, sending a prize crew aboard her, with orders to sail her to Germany. She made it as far as Tromsø in Norway, but the neutral Norwegians sent her out to sea again.

Next, the *City of Flint* headed to Murmansk, where the same thing happened. The British were now in pursuit, and eventually she was driven into the Norwegian waters again, where her German prize crew were interned. Eventually, the freighter was allowed to return to the United States. She was sunk by a U-boat in January 1943.

Meanwhile, the cruise of the *Deutschland* continued. On Saturday, 14 October she came upon the small Norwegian freighter MV *Lorenz W. Hansen*, of 1,918 tons. Although a neutral

ship, she was on her way from New Brunswick in Canada to Britain, with a cargo of timber. This made her a legitimate prize. After her crew were removed and taken on board the *Deutschland*, Thiele ordered the freighter to be sunk. It appears that for some unrecorded reason three Norwegians were lost during this scuttling. A few hours later, another merchant ship was sighted, and Thiele overhauled her. She turned out to be the Danish ship MT *Kongsdal*, on her way from South America to Denmark. A true neutral, she was protected by international law; Thiele let her go on her way, after transferring his Norwegian prisoners to her.

The *Panzerschiff Deutschland*, firing her guns at the SS *Stonegate* on 5 October 1939. The British merchant ship was en route from Chile to Egypt when she was stopped. Kapitän August Thiele allowed the British crew to abandon ship before sinking her.

As the *Lorenz W. Hansen* never sent out a radio message, the British and Norwegians did not learn of her sinking by the *Deutschland* until 21 October, when the *Kongsdal* put in to Kirkwall in Orkney, having been stopped and searched by British warships. By then, the *Deutschland* was back in her supply area off Cape Farewell. Thiele knew that the British and French were searching for her along the main convoy routes, and it made sense to lay low until the hunters returned to port. The searchers included a small French force built around the fast battleship *Dunkerque*, which had the speed and firepower to destroy the *Deutschland* if she could only bring her to bay. Instead, atrocious winter weather protected the German raider, rendering the search for her all but impossible.

By then the *Deutschland* was having problems of her own. Faults had developed with her diesel propulsion system, which could only be fixed in port. So, on 1 November the SKL recalled the *Deutschland* to Germany. Thiele headed northwards, skirting the eastern coast of Greenland, and headed home by way of the Denmark Strait. By 8 November he was safely through this key choke point, and three days later the cruiser was in the Arctic Sea, to the west of North Cape, the northernmost tip of Norway. She then headed south into the Norwegian Sea, again taking advantage of the bad weather to screen her move. She passed through the Northern Passage on the night of 13–14 November, and safely reached the Skagerrak. She finally reached Gotenhafen (now Gdynia) on Wednesday, 15 November.

The battleship *Scharnhorst*, pictured off Kiel in 1939. This is how she looked in November 1939, when she and her sister ship *Gneisenau* sortied into the Faeroes gap, to test the strength of British patrols in this key gateway into the Atlantic.

While the *Deutschland*'s cruise was unspectacular, having sunk only two ships and captured a third, it had been successful in that Thiele had managed to avoid any contact with enemy warships. His safe transits through the Northern Passage and the Denmark Strait showed that this could be done safely, especially if the raider captain timed the passage well and took full advantage of local weather conditions. The *Graf Spee* was less fortunate. Although she sank nine merchant ships totalling over 50,000 tons, she was cornered off the River Plate on 13 December and driven into the neutral port of Montevideo. Four days later, Langsdorff elected to scuttle his ship rather than risk the lives of his crew in a one-sided fight to the death. One result of this was that it led Hitler to order the renaming of the *Deutschland*, as he didn't want to risk losing a ship with so prestigious a name. Instead, she was renamed the *Lützow*.

Admiral Marschall's sortie with *Scharnhorst* and *Gneisenau*

Although the battleships *Gneisenau* and *Scharnhorst* joined the fleet well before the outbreak of war, they still had to undergo an extensive evaluation and sea trials, followed by an equally rigorous phase of crew training. *Gneisenau* had been rushed into service in 1938, before her fitting out was fully complete. This was largely due to political reasons. It wasn't until she'd served as the imposing fleet flagship in Kiel in early August that she was released to begin her trials in earnest. These led to her returning to Kiel for modifications, including the fitting of a stylish 'clipper bow'. *Scharnhorst* was completed in January 1939, but her acceptance trials and initial sea trials continued until May. After a number of modifications were made, she was finally released for service in late August, just before the outbreak of war. Meanwhile, her sister *Gneisenau* had spent six weeks cruising in the Atlantic, venturing as far south as the Azores.

When the war began, both battleships were anchored together off Brunsbüttel – the western end of the Kaiser Wilhelm (Kiel) Canal. On

Monday, 4 September, they were subjected to a bombing raid by the RAF – their first taste of action. No hits were scored, but it prompted the SKL to order them through the canal to Kiel, where they could be better protected. In this respect they were luckier than the armoured cruiser *Admiral Scheer*, which was bombed as she lay off Wilhelmshaven. She was hit once, but the bomb failed to explode. However, the light cruiser *Emden* was badly damaged as a stricken bomber

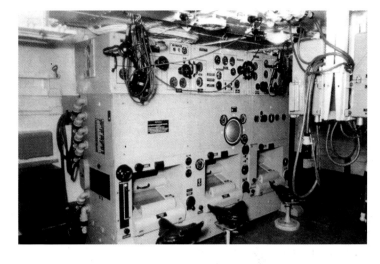

The gunnery plotting room on a German battleship – in this case the KMS *Bismarck*. The use of this Hazemeyer analog computer, coupled with information fed to it from the ship's high-quality optical rangefinders, produced accurate firing solutions for the battleship's main guns.

deliberately crashed into her. This served as a warning to Raeder to better protect the fleet's ports. In early October, the *Gneisenau* and the light cruiser *Köln* put to sea, accompanied by a screen of destroyers. They ventured as far north as Utsira, a Norwegian island on the same latitude as Orkney, before pulling back into the Skagerrak and so on to Kiel. This was merely an abortive attempt to draw the Home Fleet within range of German bombers.

By November, both battleships were in Wilhelmshaven, where their new fleet commander, Admiral Marschall, flying his flag in *Gneisenau*, was preparing for another sortie. This would serve two purposes. First, it would test the strength of the Northern Patrol, and then probe the British screens guarding the entrances into the Atlantic. Ideally, it would also prevent the British from sending more ships into the South Atlantic, to join the hunt for the *Graf Spee*. In his orders of 13 November, Raeder went so far as to command them to 'roll up enemy control of the sea passage between the Faeroes and Iceland'. This, however, wouldn't be followed by a breakout into the Atlantic. Instead, as Raeder put it, Marschall would 'feint at penetration of the North Atlantic' and so 'appear to threaten his seaborne traffic'. So, at 1310hrs on Tuesday, 21 November, the two battleships left Wilhelmshaven and headed north.

The *Scharnhorst* engaging the armed merchant cruiser *Rawalpindi*, November 1939

In November 1939, the battleships *Gneisenau* and *Scharnhorst* were ordered to probe the British defences of the Faeroes gap, between the Faeroes and Iceland. At 1607hrs on 23 November, lookouts on the *Scharnhorst* spotted smoke to the north. They turned to investigate, and came upon HMS *Rawalpindi*, an armed merchant cruiser. Her eight obsolete 6-inch guns were no match for the 28cm guns on the battleship, but when the Germans fired a warning shot, Captain Kennedy of the *Rawalpindi* fired back. *Scharnhorst* immediately replied in kind. Three minutes later a salvo of 28cm (11in.) shells crashed into the *Rawalpindi*, wrecking her bridge and cutting out her electrical power. This uneven contest continued for another 11 minutes. By the time *Gneisenau* came within range it was almost all over, although the German flagship still managed to fire a few salvoes at the stricken target, just as darkness was falling. After *Rawalpindi* sank, both battleships tried to pick up survivors. In the end, only 38 of *Rawalpindi*'s 376-strong crew survived the battle. This plate shows the engagement as it reached its climax, seconds after *Scharnhorst* scored her first hits. The *Rawalpindi* can be seen firing back, but this fire is beginning to slacken as casualties mount, and fires spread over the merchant cruiser's upper deck.

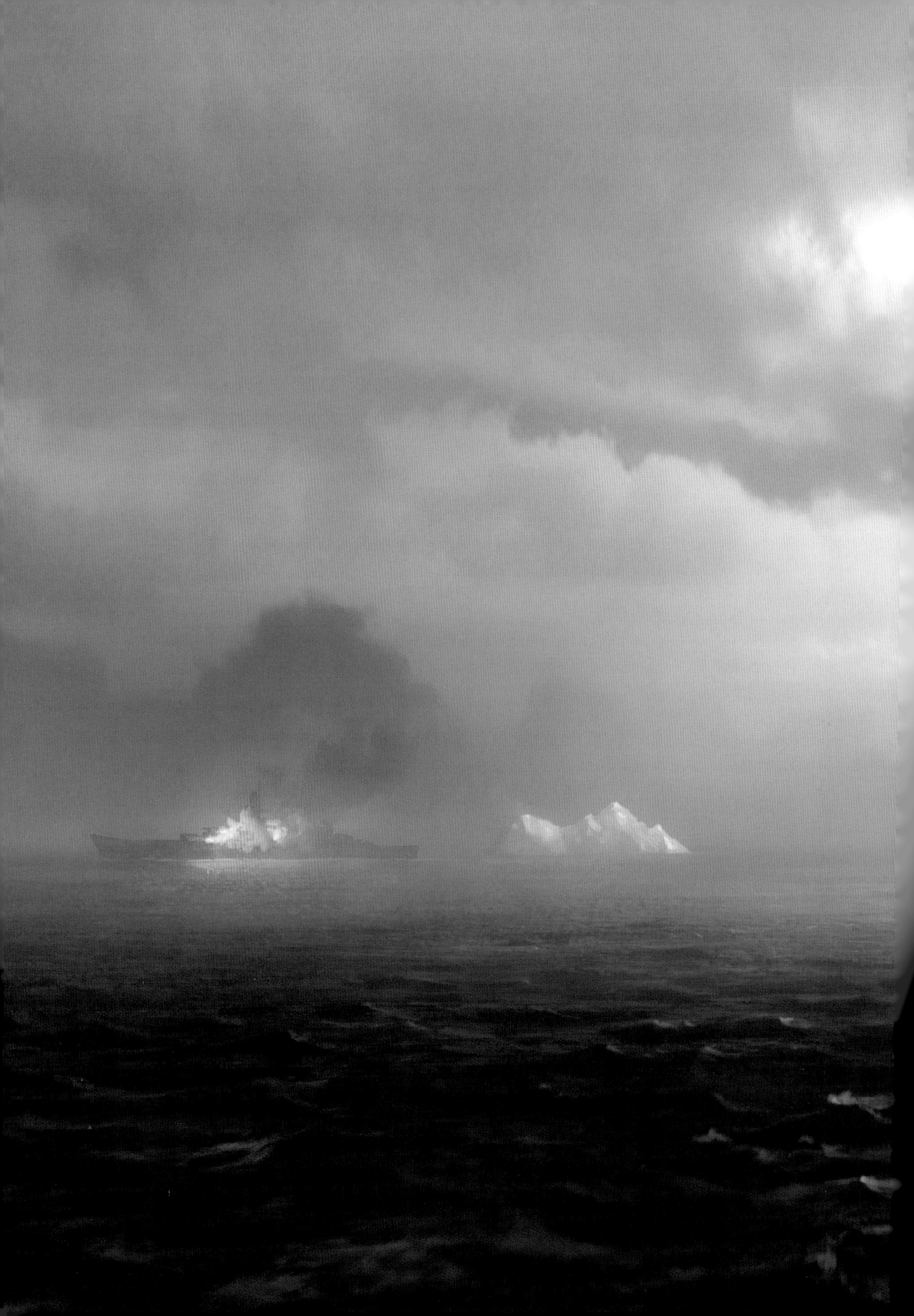

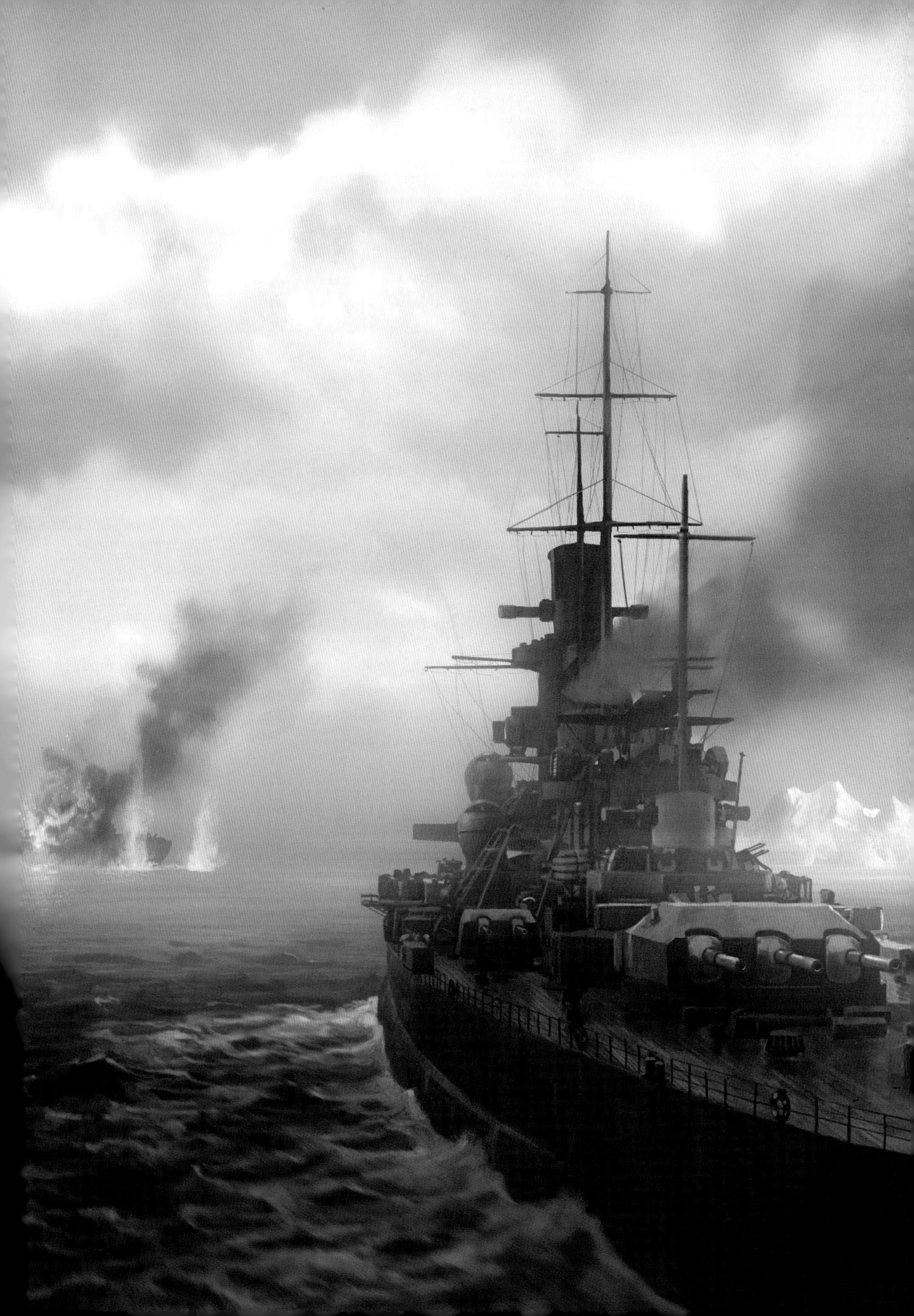

By dawn on 22 November they were passing Utsira, but this time they kept on towards the north-west, towards the Norwegian Sea. At that point, their Scouting Force of two light cruisers and three destroyers broke off and returned to port. That meant they were drawing close to the Northern Patrol, which had been moved north slightly, so it lay to the east of Shetland. However, most of the patrolling warships were away at the time, and the two battleships slipped past the remainder in daylight without being detected, thanks to poor visibility, low storm clouds and a rapidly building gale. The new battleships were rolling heavily, and many of the young, inexperienced sailors were seasick. Still, the gale abated during the night, and dawn on Thursday, 23 November revealed calm seas and good visibility. They were now to the north of the Faeroes, at the eastern end of the Faeroes gap. So far everything had gone according to plan. The real test, though, lay ahead.

At 0800hrs Marschall turned on to a north-westerly course, so his ships were running across the gap, as if steaming towards Iceland. His intention, after all, was to test the British defences, not to break through undetected. He expected a line of British cruisers and auxiliary cruisers ahead of him, but what he didn't realize was that these still lay about 50 nautical miles farther west. The light cruisers *Newcastle*, *Delhi*, *Calypso* and *Ceres* were actually spaced out in a line, parallel to Marschall's new course. However, they weren't the only British ships on patrol that day. The sea remained calm, and visibility was still good, although the German lookouts could see a fog bank to the north of them, as well as several icebergs. With twilight just over an hour away, and darkness half an hour after that, it looked like this sweep of the Faeroes gap might have been disappointingly uneventful. If it was, Marschall intended to withdraw to the east during the night, then try his luck the following morning.

At the time, the two battleships were spread out, with *Scharnhorst* 10 nautical miles to the north of *Gneisenau*. That way, Marschall could search a wider area. Then, at 1607hrs, *Scharnhorst*'s lookouts sighted smoke to the north. The battleship's commander, Kapitän Hoffmann, altered course to investigate. He signalled the flagship, 'Large steamer sighted on a parallel course, distance over 250 hundred. Have changed course to 355°.' That meant the target was 25,000m away from *Scharnhorst* – roughly 13½ nautical miles. It was still invisible to the men on board the *Gneisenau*. Marschall duly ordered his flag captain Kapitän Förste to turn the *Gneisenau* to starboard, and to follow her sister ship. On the *Scharnhorst*, with her propellers churning her along at over 30 knots, Hoffmann and his bridge staff kept their eyes on the steamer as the range dropped. He soon identified her as an armed merchant cruiser – one of the many British merchant vessels pressed into service as auxiliary warships.

This merchant cruiser was actually the 16,700-ton armed merchant cruiser *Rawalpindi*, commanded by Captain Kennedy. Her eight 6-inch guns meant she was hopelessly outmatched; so, realizing the approaching ship was a powerful German raider, Kennedy turned away to the north. Still, the German battleship had twice the speed of her quarry, and by 1640hrs the *Scharnhorst* was close enough to signal her to stop and identify herself. Kennedy sent out the random message 'FAM', designed to buy time, ordered smoke floats to be thrown overboard, to screen his ship, but these didn't work as effectively as he'd hoped – the smoke didn't billow out fast enough. The *Rawalpindi* did at least manage to send off a radio message, warning the Home Fleet that a German raider was on the loose. In the message, Kennedy incorrectly identified her as a Deutschland class. He had hoped to reach the cover of the fog bank, but as the enemy ship drew closer, he realized he was losing the race.

The battleship *Gneisenau*, pictured from her sister ship *Scharnhorst* during training exercises in the Baltic. When the two battleships operated together, it was *Gneisenau* that acted as the force flagship, flying the flag of the Kriegsmarine's fleet commander.

Then, at 1703hrs, Hoffmann gave the order to open fire. The range was now down to just 4 nautical miles. The first salvo was from a single main gun – a warning shot across the bows of the *Rawalpindi*. Realizing he wouldn't make the fog bank unscathed, Kennedy turned his ship to port, towards a nearby iceberg. He also gave orders to shoot. This was a largely symbolic gesture – his 6in. guns had no real chance of damaging the *Scharnhorst*. The salvo landed astern of the German battleship; seeing this, Hoffmann promptly issued the order to fire full salvoes. A few seconds later, the six forward main guns of the *Scharnhorst* barked out, and Hoffmann turned his ship slightly to port, so his after main turret could bear too. Then, against all the odds, *Rawalpindi*'s gunners scored a hit. Kennedy had turned his ship again to throw off the German gunners, and this time a 6in. shell from one of his starboard guns struck the German battleship on her quarterdeck.

The only damage was a gouging of the pristine wooden deck planking, and three sailors were injured by flying splinters and shrapnel. But the *Scharnhorst* had been firing too, from all three turrets, and at 1706hrs her salvo straddled the British merchant cruiser. One of the shells struck the boat deck just below the bridge, destroying the radio room and killing or wounding most of the bridge crew. Although wounded, Captain Kennedy was determined to fight on, but this wasn't easy. The *Rawalpindi*'s rudimentary optical fire control had been knocked out by the hit, along with one of the starboard guns. Electrical power was also cut, so the guns could now only be loaded by hand. It was clear that time was fast running out for the *Rawalpindi*.

Over the next few minutes, the German shells continued to strike the hapless merchant cruiser. By that time the *Gneisenau* had appeared in sight to the east, and she too began opening up on the British ship. The *Rawalpindi*'s steering gear was destroyed, forcing her to turn in lazy circles, and fires had now broken out fore and aft. She was losing steam power too.

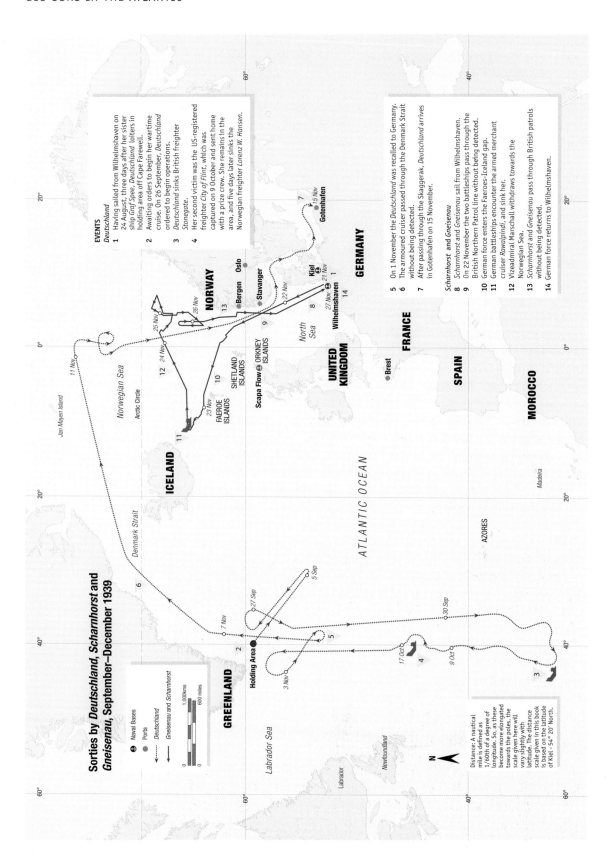

Sorties by *Deutschland*, *Scharnhorst* and *Gneisenau*, September–December 1939

EVENTS

Deutschland

1 Having sailed from Wilhelmshaven on 24 August, three days after her sister ship *Graf Spee*, *Deutschland* loiters in holding area off Cape Farewell.

2 Awaiting orders to begin her wartime cruise. On 26 September, *Deutschland* ordered to begin operations.

3 *Deutschland* sinks British freighter *Stonegate*.

4 Her second victim was the US-registered freighter *City of Flint*, which was captured on 9 October and sent home with a prize crew. She remains in the area, and five days later sinks the Norwegian freighter *Lorenz W. Hansen*.

Scharnhorst and Gneisenau

5 On 1 November the *Deutschland* was recalled to Germany.

6 The armoured cruiser passed through the Denmark Strait without being detected.

7 After passing through the Skaggerak, *Deutschland* arrives in Gotenhafen on 15 November.

8 *Scharnhorst* and *Gneisenau* sail from Wilhelmshaven.

9 On 22 November the two battleships pass through the British Northern Patrol line without being detected.

10 German force enters the Faeroes–Iceland gap.

11 German battleships encounter the armed merchant cruiser *Rawalpindi*, and sink her.

12 Vizeadmiral Marschall withdraws towards the Norwegian Sea.

13 *Scharnhorst* and *Gneisenau* pass through British patrols without being detected.

14 German force returns to Wilhelmshaven.

Distance: A nautical mile is defined as 1/60th of a degree of longitude. So, as these become more elongated towards the poles, the scale given here will vary slightly with latitude. The distance scale given in this book is based on the latitude of Kiel – 54° 20' North.

Naval Bases
Ports
Deutschland
Gneisenau and Scharnhorst

0   1,000kms
0   600 miles

N

One by one, the guns were knocked out, mainly by shell splinters, and the bridge was hit again. By this time, the courageous Captain Kennedy was dead, and it was one of his surviving officers who finally gave the order to abandon ship. Boats were lowered, but one was capsized and damaged by a German shell landing nearby. It was now almost pitch dark, so the blazing ship was visible for miles. It was by this light that the Germans watched the final moments of the engagement at 1717hrs.

A fresh salvo fired from *Scharnhorst* at a range of 3 miles struck her hull at least three times, and one of the shells penetrated the *Rawalpindi*'s after magazine. The blast caused extensive damage, and the ship began heeling over to port. By then many of her British crew were already dead, but a handful managed to scramble into lifeboats, or jump clear into the icy water. Watching all this, Marschall had to weigh up the risk to his battleships against his duty as a seaman. In the end compassion won, and at 1730hrs he ordered *Scharnhorst* to 'rescue survivors'; however, this wasn't an easy task. The German battleship inched close to the port beam of the sinking ship. At least one of the lifeboats was overturned as the *Scharnhorst* manoeuvred alongside it. *Gneisenau* drew closer as well, on the *Rawalpindi*'s starboard beam. Once the merchant cruiser finally sank at around 1800hrs, both battleships used their searchlights to continue the search in the darkness.

The largely fruitless rescue mission was still under way at 1915hrs, when the radar operator on *Gneisenau* detected an unknown contact approaching from the west. It was the British light cruiser *Newcastle*, drawn to the scene by *Rawalpindi*'s radio message. Her lookouts had time to spot the glow of the fires before the *Rawalpindi* finally sank. Behind her, other cruisers from the British screen were closing in too – *Delhi*, and then the two heavy cruisers *Norfolk* and *Suffolk*. In fact, Captain Kennedy's radio message spurred the Home Fleet into immediate action, as Admiral Forbes ordered ships from

The sinking of the *Rawalpindi* in November 1941 was a baptism of fire for the crews of *Gneisenau* and *Scharnhorst*, but the action was very one-sided, as the armed merchant cruiser offered no real threat to the German battleships.

Admiral Wilhelm Marschall (1886–1976) joined the Imperial German Navy in 1906, and served as a U-boat commander during World War I. In October 1939 he became the Kriegsmarine's Flottenchef (Fleet Commander), and so commanded *Gneisenau* and *Scharnhorst* during their probe of the Faeroes gap in November 1939. In June 1940, after a mediocre performance in the Norwegian campaign, he was replaced as fleet commander by Günther Lütjens.

as far apart as the Denmark Strait and the River Clyde to join the hunt for the German battleships. When the sighting was reported to Marschall, he ordered both ships to douse all lights, and speed off towards the east.

The *Newcastle* saw them go and tried to follow, before losing them in the darkness and the fog bank that was now creeping southwards. *Scharnhorst* even laid a smokescreen to cover her tracks. The British cruiser's commander Captain Figgins eventually broke off contact and returned to search for survivors. In the end, 38 of the *Rawalpindi*'s crew were rescued, most by the *Scharnhorst*, and the rest by British ships. Captain Kennedy and most of his crew of 276 men went down with their ship. It was a futile, one-sided action, but it probably wasn't fought in vain. The gallant defence of the *Rawalpindi* convinced Marschall that more powerful British warships were nearby. Why would Kennedy fight such a hopeless action, other than to delay the Germans long enough for the Home Fleet to intercept them? So, he decided that honour had been served. His ships had tested the British defences as ordered, and so had accomplished their mission.

The weather continued to deteriorate during the night. As the two German battleships sped off to the east, with *Gneisenau* leading *Scharnhorst*, the crews found themselves battering their way through a gale. Still, at midnight Marschall ordered another course change – a turn towards the north-east. He was convinced the Home Fleet was in hot pursuit, even though its capital ships were still well out of reach. In fact, Forbes, with the battleships *Nelson* and *Rodney*, plus the heavy cruiser *Devonshire*, had only left the Clyde that evening, and it would be Saturday before they reached the latitude of the Faeroes. Out in the Atlantic, the battleship *Warspite* was ordered north to cover the Denmark Strait, while the battlecruiser *Repulse* and the carrier *Furious* were also ordered to break off from the convoys they were escorting and head towards Scapa Flow. Forbes also ordered the Northern Patrol screen to be moved north to just above the latitude off Bergen and sent extra cruisers to reinforce it.

Admiral Marschall had expected this. So, he spent most of Friday and Saturday in the Arctic Ocean, biding his time and hoping the Home Fleet would start running low on fuel and so return to port. The atrocious weather was doing little for the wellbeing of his crews, but at least it was helping to hide his striking force. In the meantime, the SKL had been monitoring British radio traffic and had deduced that the British still thought there were two German raiders at large, one being the *Deutschland*. Kiel duly signalled *Gneisenau* with the news: 'British Home Fleet at sea since 1800hrs. *Delhi* and *Newcastle* attached from Northern Patrol. Destroyers in Firth of Forth at three hours' notice.' For Marschall, this all meant that he'd no chance of repeating his probe of the Faeroes gap.

On the afternoon of 24 November, Forbes signalled all ships with the news: '*Deutschland* and second unidentified warship currently located north of Iceland, waiting for excitement provoked by their appearance to subside. It is reasonable to hope, however, that these ships may never reach Germany.' So, the Home Fleet might not have known what ships they were facing, but they had a reasonable idea where they were. Marschall, however, had an ally in the weather. An even greater storm was gathering off Greenland. Dr Hartung, the fleet meteorologist, predicted the weather front would reach the Norwegian coast by the morning of Sunday, 27 November. The German fleet commander gambled on this forecast and waited a little before giving the order to head south. Sure enough, the strong south-westerly gale began lashing the Norwegian coast, bringing with it driving rain and wretched visibility. For Marschall, this was the perfect storm.

At dawn on 26 November, the two German battleships were passing Stadlandet in Norway, a hundred nautical miles north of Bergen. This is where they should have encountered the Northern Patrol, now reinforced by two heavy cruisers (*Norfolk* and *Suffolk*), five light cruisers (*Glasgow*, *Southampton*, *Newcastle*, *Sheffield* and *Edinburgh*) and seven destroyers. Four hours' steaming to the west was the main body of the Home Fleet, with *Nelson*, *Rodney* and *Devonshire*. In the end, despite this closely woven net, the two German ships slipped through without being detected. By noon they were safely past the Northern Passage and, still keeping close to the Norwegian coast, they were approaching the Utsira lighthouse. The same bad weather also shielded them from the British submarines lying off the entrance to the Skagerrak, and so the final leg of the voyage was uneventful. The two battleships arrived safely in Wilhelmshaven shortly before noon on Monday morning, 27 November.

Afterwards, the SKL portrayed the sortie as a great success: 'The appearance of our battleships in the Faeroe Islands region has demonstrated that the enemy, despite his superiority, is incapable of maintaining command of the sea round his own shores.' In fact, the German sortie was a hesitant and feeble attempt to probe the Royal Navy's defensive cordon. While the British lost an armed merchant cruiser, Admiral Marschall had failed to push his way through the Faeroes gap to reach the North Atlantic beyond. Instead, his two powerful German capital ships had withdrawn when threatened by nothing more powerful than a solitary British light cruiser. However, Marschall rode out the criticism and was retained as the Kriegsmarine's senior fleet admiral until after the Norwegian campaign of 1940. Few knew it at the time, but after the Faeroes gap venture, it would be almost a year before another Atlantic sortie was attempted.

The *Admiral Scheer's* sortie

The reason for this hiatus was Hitler's latest phase of military conquest. By early 1940, he was planning the invasion of France and the Low Countries. Then, Grossadmiral Raeder suggested an expansion of this campaign, to encompass Norway and Denmark. For the Kriegsmarine this made good sense. It offered his ships and U-boats bases along the Norwegian coast, which could be protected from attack by coastal defences, supported by the Luftwaffe. There was also the fear that the Allies would pre-empt them, to secure access to Swedish iron ore and deny Germany its use. So, when Hitler agreed, plans were drawn up for this invasion, which was codenamed Operation *Weserübung*. The Kriegsmarine would be fully committed to the operation, protecting the invasion forces and keeping the Royal Navy at bay.

The invasion began on 9 April 1940. The Germans soon found out it was a less straightforward operation than they had anticipated. Norwegian resistance was tougher than expected, and Allied intervention more effective. Eventually, though, the Luftwaffe helped turn the tide, and by June the Allies were forced to evacuate their remaining troops. Norway had been captured, but the cost to the Kriegsmarine had been high. It lost three cruisers (*Blücher*, *Königsberg* and *Karlsruhe*), as well as ten destroyers. Several warships had been damaged too, including *Scharnhorst*, *Gneisenau* and *Lützow*, while during this period both *Admiral Scheer* and *Prinz Eugen* were damaged in air attacks on German ports. So, by the summer of 1940, the Kriegsmarine was in no shape to take any large-scale offensive action. Effectively, only the *Admiral Hipper* was available for commerce-raiding operations.

On 10 May, Germany invaded France, Belgium and the Netherlands. The operation proved a stunning success, and in less than two weeks the German panzers had reached the Channel coast. A large portion of the remaining Allied forces found themselves trapped against the coast, prompting the mass evacuation of troops from Dunkirk and Boulogne. By the end of June, over 330,000 British and French troops had been saved from capture, but the Germans were now free to drive on towards Paris. The French capital fell on 14 June, and a week later the French capitulated, signing an armistice. On 10 June Italy entered the war and launched its own limited invasion of southern France. The country was now divided in two, with a zone of German occupation to the north, and a zone of Italian occupation

The issuing of hot food on board German raiders was done by individual messes. A representative from each mess would collect the food from the galley in a pot, which he then took back to his mess table where it would be served out.

in the south. What this meant for the Kriegsmarine was that it now had access to the French Atlantic ports of Brest and Saint-Nazaire. This would dramatically change the strategic situation in the North Atlantic.

It was autumn before Hitler allowed the Kriegsmarine to take advantage of all this. He had been holding it in readiness for an invasion of Britain, but when the Luftwaffe failed to defeat the Royal Air Force in the Battle of Britain, the invasion was postponed, and then quietly cancelled. During the spring and summer of 1940, the Germans had sent commerce raiders into the Atlantic – a handful of *Hilfskreuzer* (armed merchant ships), most of which went

on to hunt in the South Atlantic or Indian Ocean. These achieved moderate success, but they lacked the strength to take on the transatlantic convoys. So, Raeder was keen to send a more powerful commerce raider into the Atlantic. His options of ships were limited due to the losses and damage caused during the Norway campaign, but the *Panzerschiff Admiral Scheer* had nearly completed her month-long post-refit exercises in the Baltic, and so would be ready to sortie by mid-October. She, then, would spearhead the Kriegsmarine's return to the Atlantic. Ironically, this long cruise would be codenamed Operation *Nordseetour*.

The *Panzerschiff* sailed from Gotenhafen on 23 October and headed west to Kiel. From there, after taking on final stores and orders, Kapitän Theodor Krancke conned her through the Kaiser Wilhelm Canal, to enter the estuary of the River Elbe. This conveniently bypassed the known British submarine patrols operating in the mouth of the Skagerrak. From there, the *Admiral Scheer* left Brunsbüttel on Monday, 27 October, and slipped into the North Sea. The following day, Krancke briefly put in to the Norwegian coast near Stavanger to wait for a covering weather front to appear, then resumed his voyage north that afternoon. British reconnaissance flights didn't spot the cruiser as she passed through the Northern Passage, and by that evening she was out of danger, heading north through the Norwegian Sea. Planning to avoid the Faeroes gap, at midnight Krancke turned towards the north-west, on a course which would take him around the north of Iceland.

Krancke's timing was perfect. On Friday, 31 October, he passed through the Denmark Strait without being detected and so entered the North Atlantic. He followed the eastern course of Greenland, hugging the edge of the seasonal pack ice before turning south when he reached the latitude of Cape Farewell. His intention was to prey on the Halifax to Britain convoy route, keeping roughly a thousand miles from the Canadian port. So far, thanks to good security and radio silence, the British had no

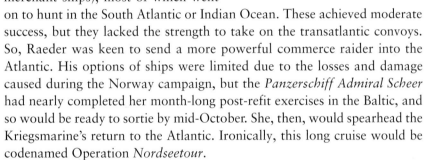

The Deutschland-class armoured ship *Admiral Scheer*, pictured during a courtesy visit to Gibraltar before the war. Her extended commerce-raiding cruise in 1940–41 took her as far as the South Atlantic and the Indian Ocean, but she first made her mark in the North Atlantic, when she attacked Convoy HX-84.

inkling the *Panzerschiff* was at sea. So, her sudden appearance would come as a profound shock.

At 1430hrs on Wednesday, 5 November, she came across a lone freighter, the SS *Mopan* of 5,389 tons, which Krancke presumed was a straggler from a nearby convoy. A banana boat, she was actually sailing alone between the Caribbean and Britain when she was stopped. The sudden appearance of the German cruiser took the crew by surprise, and they heeded the stern warning not to transmit a distress signal. Instead, the 72-man crew were transferred to the *Admiral Scheer*, and the *Mopan* was sunk using the ship's secondary 10.5cm guns. This, though, was not the victim Krancke had been looking for. *B-Dienst* intercepts had suggested that a convoy was close by, and with dusk approaching he feared it might get away. So, as soon as the banana boat was sunk at 1605hrs, the German cruiser set off in pursuit of the convoy. Had the *Mopan* sent off a message, she might have given the homeward-bound convoy a chance to escape.

Convoy HX-84 consisted of 37 merchant ships, but it was only lightly protected by three aged destroyers and the armed merchant cruiser HMS *Jervis Bay*. At the time the *Admiral Scheer* appeared it was at 52° 45' North, 32° 13' West, some 1,300 nautical miles west of Halifax, steaming east at 8 knots, with its 37 ships arrayed in nine columns and five rows. In other words, the convoy was formed up in a big rectangle, almost 5 miles wide and a mile and a half deep. The *Jervis Bay* was just ahead of it, near its north-eastern corner, while the destroyers were on the opposite southern end of the box. For Captain Edward Fegen of the *Jervis Bay*, the first sign of trouble was a floatplane, which appeared to the north-west of the convoy, off its port quarter, at 1555hrs. This could only have come from a warship, but it was too far away to identify as either friend or foe. Fegen peeled his ship away from the convoy to investigate.

Minutes later, he spotted smoke on the north-western horizon. The *Jervis Bay* held its course. By 1620hrs it was visible from the bridge – a warship of some kind. He presumed it was British, as no word of a German raider at large had reached him. The range was now 15 nautical miles. The two ships closed with each other, one making 12 knots, the other 28. As they drew closer, Fegen flashed out a request for the approaching ship to identify herself. Kapitän Krancke repeated the same 'MAG' signal back to the British ship. Then, at 1640hrs, when the two ships were just 12 miles apart, Krancke slowed his ship to a crawl, turned her to port, and so unmasked his real identity. On board the *Jervis Bay*, the shock that they were facing a 'pocket battleship' was followed by a grim determination to fight. First, Fegen ordered the convoy to scatter towards the south-east. Then, he radioed the Admiralty, saying, 'One battleship, bearing 328°, distance 12 miles', and gave his position. This was the first the British knew that a German raider was at sea.

Moments later, the *Admiral Scheer* at 1642hrs opened fire with two of her 28cm (11in.) guns. This first ranging salvo fell 200m short. The *Jervis Bay* turned to port too, to expose her full starboard broadside. She also dropped smoke floats, to help screen the convoy's escape. So, the ships were

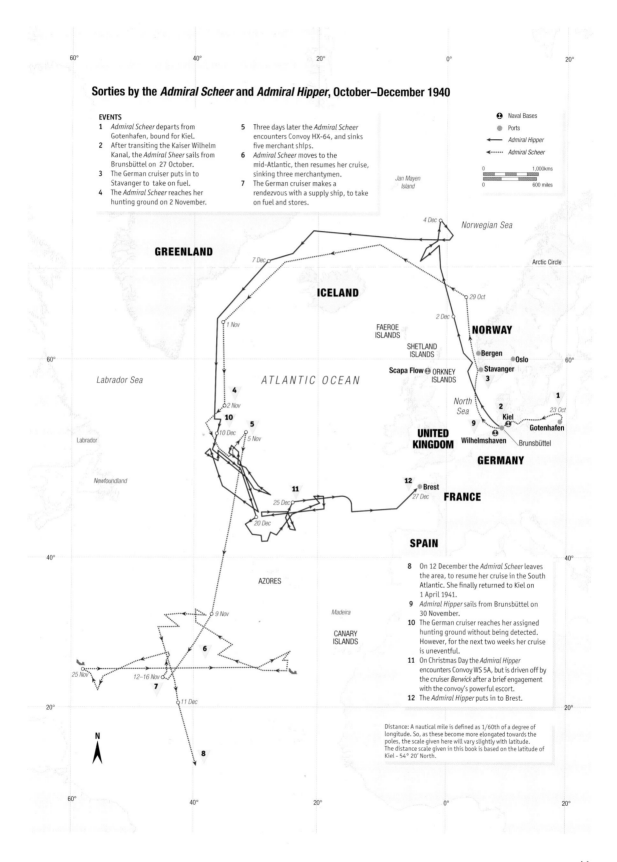

Sorties by the *Admiral Scheer* and *Admiral Hipper*, October–December 1940

EVENTS

1 *Admiral Scheer* departs from Gotenhafen, bound for Kiel.
2 After transiting the Kaiser Wilhelm Kanal, the *Admiral Sheer* sails from Brunsbüttel on 27 October.
3 The German cruiser puts in to Stavanger to take on fuel.
4 The *Admiral Scheer* reaches her hunting ground on 2 November.
5 Three days later the *Admiral Scheer* encounters Convoy HX-64, and sinks five merchant ships.
6 *Admiral Scheer* moves to the mid-Atlantic, then resumes her cruise, sinking three merchantymen.
7 The German cruiser makes a rendezvous with a supply ship, to take on fuel and stores.

8 On 12 December the *Admiral Scheer* leaves the area, to resume her cruise in the South Atlantic. She finally returned to Kiel on 1 April 1941.
9 *Admiral Hipper* sails from Brunsbüttel on 30 November.
10 The German cruiser reaches her assigned hunting ground without being detected. However, for the next two weeks her cruise is uneventful.
11 On Christmas Day the *Admiral Hipper* encounters Convoy WS 5A, but is driven off by the cruiser *Berwick* after a brief engagement with the convoy's powerful escort.
12 The *Admiral Hipper* puts in to Brest.

Naval Bases
Ports
Admiral Hipper
Admiral Scheer

0   1,000kms
0   600 miles

Distance: A nautical mile is defined as 1/60th of a degree of longitude. So, as these become more elongated towards the poles, the scale given here will vary slightly with latitude. The distance scale given in this book is based on the latitude of Kiel - 54° 20′ North.

GREENLAND
ICELAND
Jan Mayen Island
Norwegian Sea
Arctic Circle
FAEROE ISLANDS
SHETLAND ISLANDS
Scapa Flow ORKNEY ISLANDS
NORWAY
Bergen
Oslo
Stavanger
North Sea
ATLANTIC OCEAN
Labrador Sea
Labrador
Newfoundland
UNITED KINGDOM
Kiel
Gotenhafen
Wilhelmshaven
Brunsbüttel
GERMANY
Brest
FRANCE
SPAIN
AZORES
Madeira
CANARY ISLANDS

29 Oct
23 Oct
2 Dec
4 Dec
7 Dec
1 Nov
2 Nov
10 Dec
5 Nov
25 Dec
20 Dec
11 Dec
9 Nov
25 Nov
12–16 Nov
27 Dec

N

The armed merchant cruiser *Jervis Bay*, pictured in Dakar in either January or April 1940. Until her loss, she was painted in her company colour scheme of a green hull, white superstructure and buff funnel. In this photograph the 6in. (15cm) gun in her starboard waist can be seen, trained aft.

almost parallel to each other, 12 miles apart, with the German cruiser edging closer in. The two protagonists were locked in a duel which could only have one outcome. The *Jervis Bay* returned the German fire with four 6in. guns, but her shots fell short. They were out of effective range. The converted liner also lacked the sophisticated optical fire control of her opponent. The next two shells from *Admiral Scheer* straddled the target, peppering her decks with pieces of shrapnel thrown up when the shells burst in the sea around the British ship.

The third salvo – a full one of six shells – was fired at 1644hrs, and it also straddled the *Jervis Bay*. One of these shells hit near the merchant cruiser's bridge, and shrapnel also sliced across her decks. This was only the start of what would amount to a demolition of the former liner. The *Admiral Scheer* scored at least two hits with her fourth salvo, and fires broke out on the merchant cruiser's splintered deck. By now her rangefinder had been destroyed, so what guns remained in action were firing individually. The next few minutes saw the liner pounded into scrap. According to the German gunners it was the fifth salvo, fired at 1645hrs, that all but tore the British ship apart. Survivors recall her deck buckling with the blast, and all her guns were silenced. The *Jervis Bay* began gliding to a stop, as steam power was cut to her boilers, and fires began raging on her upper decks. She also began listing to starboard, having been hit near the waterline. Due to *Jervis Bay*'s lack of protective armour, the German shells were causing carnage below decks.

A seaman, looking up at the wrecked bridge, saw the captain with one arm partly severed. His final order was to abandon ship. Soon after that, the bridge was engulfed in flame, and Captain Fegen with it. It took just ten minutes to knock the *Jervis Bay* out of the fight. As the list increased, her surviving crew began carrying out Captain Fegen's final orders.

The *Admiral Scheer*, however, was already setting off in pursuit of the convoy, hoping to cause as much damage as she could before the approaching darkness hid the merchant ships from sight. Although his radar was temporarily out of action, Kapitän Krancke felt he could probably continue his attack in the dark. However, he suspected there would be destroyers about, and he had strict orders not to put his ship at risk of a torpedo attack.

The communications room in a Deutschland-class armoured cruiser. This was a vital tool for these powerful commerce raiders, as by monitoring traffic from Allied shipping the raider captain could build up a reasonably accurate picture of both convoy movements and the activities of enemy warships.

Meanwhile, the tragedy of the *Jervis Bay* played itself out, and the ship finally rolled over onto her side and then sank at around 1700hrs. Of her crew of 254 men, 68 survived to be rescued by the neutral Swedish steamer *Stureholm*. Three of these men would later die of their injuries.

Meanwhile, the *Admiral Scheer* was busy attacking the scattered convoy. Her first victim was the SS *Maidan*, a British freighter, which was sunk with all hands. The tanker MV *San Demetrio* was hit and set on fire, but she managed to limp away to safety, and amazingly survived to make it into the Clyde. Two more freighters were then sunk – the *Kenbane Head* and *Trewellard*. The rest of the convoy was saved by dusk, and by the sacrifice of the next victim, the SS *Beaverford*, a Canadian freighter of 10,042 tons. After seeing the *Kenbane Head* blow up, Captain Hugh Pettigrew turned the *Beaverford* towards the enemy cruiser, in an attempt to buy more time for the other merchant ships. The Scottish-born captain used the smokescreen left by the convoy to play hide and seek with his powerful hunter, firing when he could with his single 4in. gun. It was a ludicrously one-sided contest, but it occupied the *Admiral Scheer* until after nightfall.

The *Beaverford* was hit repeatedly, and eventually she was brought to a halt, with her decks on fire. At 2245hrs Krancke ordered her finished off with a torpedo. The gallant merchantman had her stern ripped off, and she sank quickly, taking all 77 of her crew with her. This sacrifice had spared

---

The *Admiral Scheer* firing at the armed merchant cruiser *Jervis Bay*, November 1940

In a scene reminiscent of the fight between *Scharnhorst* and the *Rawalpindi*, in the late afternoon of 5 November 1940, the *Admiral Scheer* found herself facing HMS *Jervis Bay*, another armed merchant cruiser. She was protecting Convoy HX-84, and steamed out to meet the *Admiral Scheer*, deliberately sacrificing herself so the convoy could escape. Kapitän Kranke turned the German cruiser so all her guns would bear, and at 1642hrs she opened fire with her 28cm (11in.) guns. The *Jervis Bay* fired back, even though her 6in. guns were still out of range. Two minutes later a German shell hit the merchant cruiser's bridge, and over the next few minutes the

British ship was reduced to a blazing wreck. The battle, such as it was, lasted less than ten minutes. The *Jervis Bay* would finally sink at 1700hrs. Only 68 of her 254-man crew would survive. The cost had been extremely high, but at least most of the convoy would escape in the darkness. The *Admiral Scheer* would sink a total of five merchant ships from the convoy that day and badly damage another. This shows the short action from the perspective of the German raider. The *Jervis Bay* has already been hit, and more German salvoes are on their way. However, behind her, the convoy can be seen escaping, its departure partly hidden by a smokescreen.

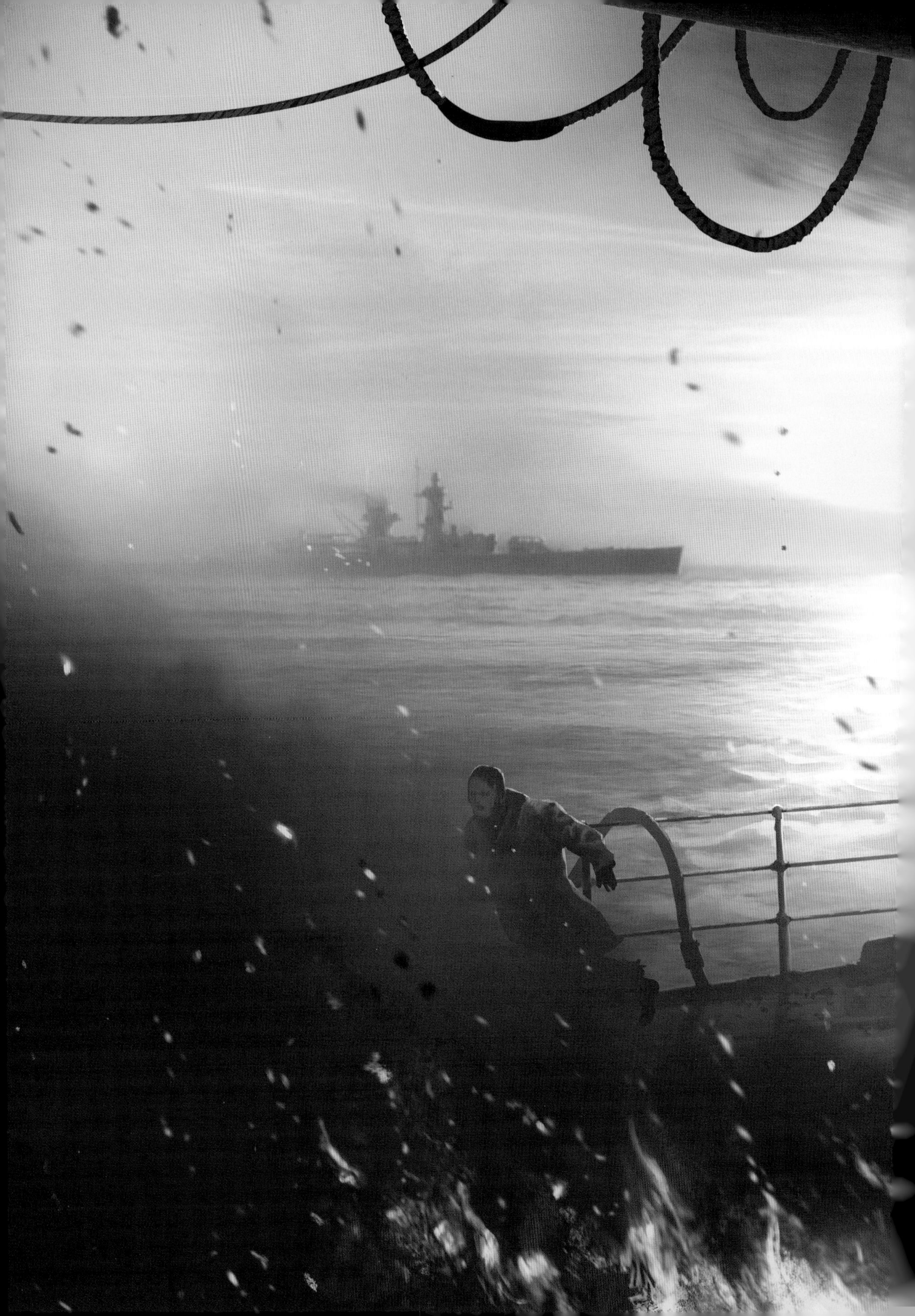

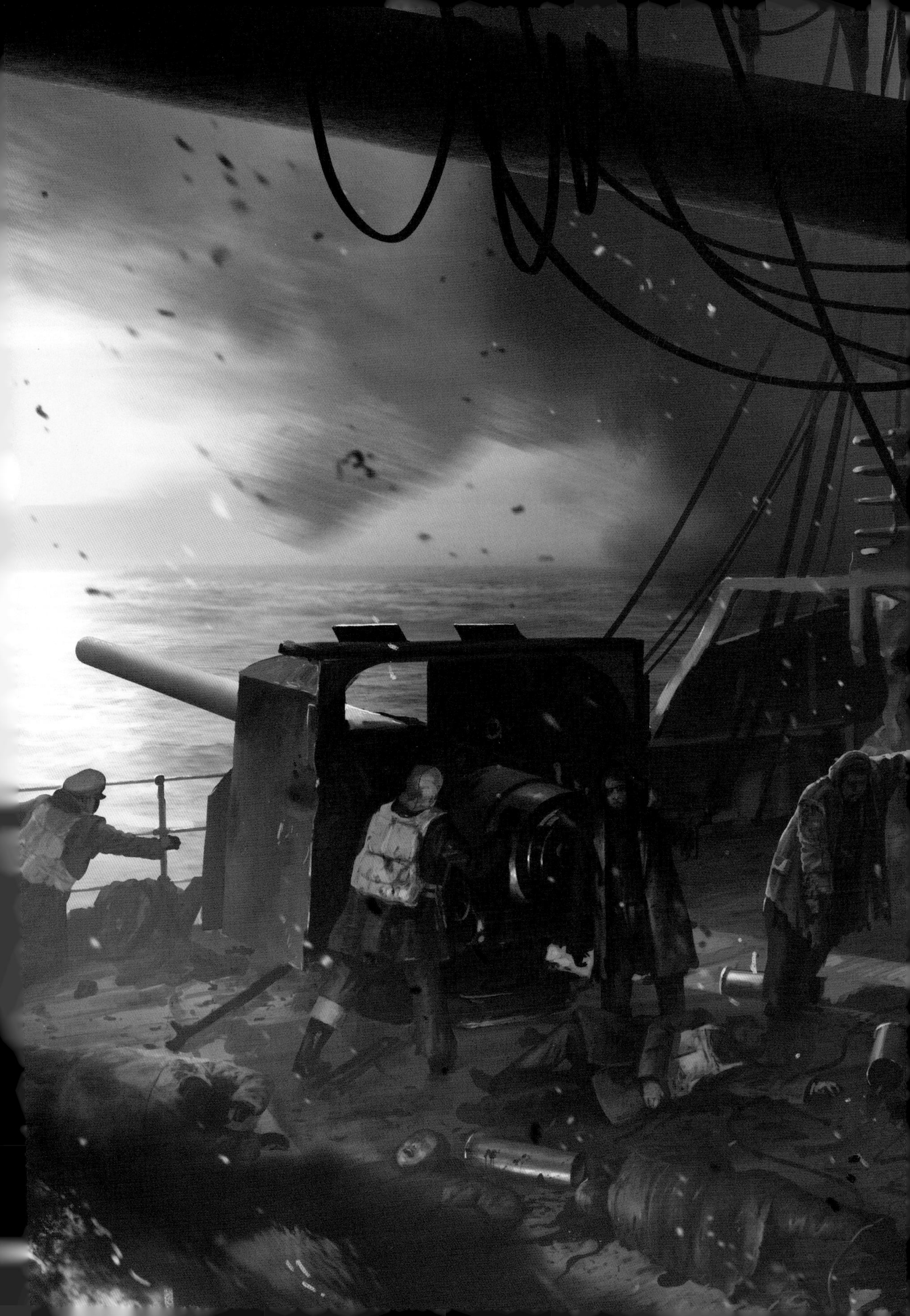

During the *Admiral Scheer*'s attack on Convoy HX-84, the tanker MV *San Demetrio* was shelled and set ablaze. She escaped, but as the fire took hold, her crew abandoned ship. Then, finding her cargo of aviation fuel hadn't blown up, they returned and nursed her into the Clyde. Their exploits were later immortalized in the film *San Demetrio London* (1943), and by this painting by Norman Wilkinson.

the convoy. It was now widely scattered, and although the *Admiral Scheer* gave chase, she only overhauled one more ship, the freighter SS *Fresno City*. Afterwards, Captain Fegen of the *Jervis Bay* was awarded a posthumous Victoria Cross. Unfortunately, the sacrifice of Captain Pettigrew and his men was never properly recognized.

Finally giving up on Convoy HX-84, Kapitän Krancke turned away to the south and began his long voyage towards the South Atlantic. The next few days were uneventful. On 12 November, the *Admiral Scheer* rendezvoused with the tanker *Eurofeld* and the supply ship *Nordmark*. He transferred his prisoners from the *Mopan* to the supply ship, and then set off on a hunt of the Atlantic between the Caribbean and West Africa along the latitude of the Tropic of Cancer. This was a singularly unprofitable time for the raider, which only managed to intercept two solitary merchant ships, on 25 November, to the north-west of Anguilla, and on 1 December, to the south-west of the Cape Verde Islands. So, on 10 December, having refuelled again from the *Eurofeld*, the *Admiral Scheer* set off into the South Atlantic. Her cruise there was a little more profitable, as was her subsequent foray into the Indian Ocean. On 3 March the German raider began her long voyage home, and she arrived back in Kiel on 1 April 1941, having slipped back through the British patrols the way she had come.

The cruise of the *Admiral Scheer* had been successful – the most profitable German commerce-raiding cruise of the entire war. Her spectacular attack on Convoy HX-84 netted six merchant ships, totalling 38,720 tons. Three more merchantmen had been damaged, including the *San Demetrio*. She also sank the armed merchant cruiser *Jervis Bay*. Then, in the South Atlantic and Indian Ocean, she sank another eight merchant ships, and captured two more. In all, she sank or captured 113,622 tons of Allied shipping. The drawback was that, after this extensive cruise, the ship had to undergo an equally extensive refit and so wouldn't be available for further operations.

By the time she re-emerged, the Kriegsmarine had completely lost its appetite for commerce raiding. However, while the *Admiral Scheer* remained at sea, and her successes mounted, Grossadmiral Raeder was determined not only to continue his Atlantic raids, but to make them even larger.

Operation *Nordseetour*

One of the problems with the Kriegsmarine's heavy cruisers was their lack of range. The Admiral Hipper class could only manage 6,500 nautical miles without refuelling. This was significantly more than the fleet's light cruisers, which effectively precluded them from acting as commerce raiders. The fall of France now gave the Kriegsmarine the opportunity to redeploy their heavy cruisers on the French Atlantic coast. That would save the dangerous voyage north around Iceland and the Faeroes, and place the ships much closer to the Atlantic convoy routes. However, in late 1940 the *Prinz Eugen* was still in Kiel, waiting to be commissioned. It would be spring 1941 before she became fully operational. With *Blücher* sunk, that left the *Admiral Hipper*. After the conquest of Norway, she remained in Norwegian waters until August 1941, when she returned to Wilhelmshaven for a refit. She was ready for action by late September.

The original plan was that she would sortie into the North Atlantic to act as a diversion, distracting the Home Fleet during Operation *Seelöwe* (*Sea Lion*), the cross-channel invasion of southern England. This diversionary sortie, codenamed Operation *Herbstreise* (*Autumn Journey*), would coincide with a fake invasion attempt on the Scottish coast, to keep the Home Fleet's attention away from the English Channel. The cancellation of *Seelöwe* also meant *Admiral Hipper*'s sortie was also stopped. Raeder saw no reason why the cruise couldn't go ahead anyway, as a stand-alone operation. On Tuesday, 24 September 1940, the cruiser left Wilhelmshaven, on what should have been the start of a commerce-raiding cruise. On its completion, the cruiser's commander Kapitän Wilhelm Meisel was ordered to put in to

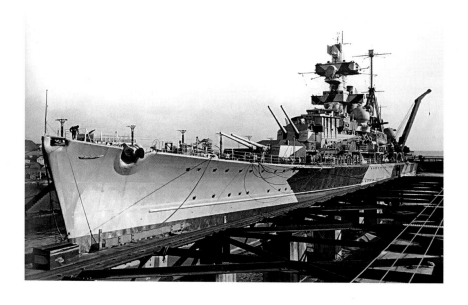

The sleek lines of the heavy cruiser *Admiral Hipper* made her fast, but these same sleek lines, coupled with her lack of endurance, made her largely unsuitable as a North Atlantic commerce raider. Still, the cruiser made three successful sorties, sinking 32,806 tons of shipping.

Brest. However, before *Admiral Hipper* cleared the coast of Denmark an engine room fire brought the operation to an abrupt end. She was forced to limp into Hamburg, where she was hurriedly repaired.

The SKL decided to continue with the operation in October. This time it would be codenamed Operation *Nordseetour*. It began on Saturday, 30 November, when the cruiser left Brunsbüttel, and steamed north towards Norway. To compensate for the cruiser's poor range, no fewer than four German tankers had already been sent out into the North Atlantic, to help feed her fuel-hungry engines. Like the *Admiral Scheer* before her, the *Admiral Hipper* put in to the Norwegian coast during daylight and clear weather, and sailed north through the internal waterways near Bergen before returning to the Norwegian Sea. She headed a little west of north until the late evening of 3 December. Then, she lingered again, this time refuelling and cruising back and forth in the Arctic Sea, waiting for another spell of poor weather. Choosing his moment perfectly, Meisel then steamed west to reach the Denmark Strait.

He passed through it without any problems during Saturday, 7 December and, like Kapitän Krancke before him, reached the North Atlantic without being detected. He followed Krancke's old course too, south-west down the eastern coast of Greenland, and then south to a rendezvous with a waiting tanker. At that point, the *Admiral Hipper* found itself overtaken by a strong gale that reached storm force. The cruiser was battered by mountainous seas, and this storm had barely eased when on 10 December the cruiser's starboard engine broke down. While his engine room crew tried to fix it, Meisel limped off at reduced speed to find his waiting tanker. Contact was finally made late in the evening of Wednesday, 11 December, by which time the cruiser was almost completely out of fuel. So, with the storm past and his fuel tanks refilled, Meisel was finally ready to begin his Atlantic cruise.

Unlike the *Admiral Scheer*'s Krancke, Kapitän Meisel of the *Admiral Hipper* had been given permission to attack enemy convoys, if they were lightly protected. He was already on the edge of the Halifax to Britain convoy route, some 1,200 nautical miles from Halifax, and not far from the spot where, just over a month before, the *Admiral Scheer* had attacked Convoy HX-84. So, he began his hunt there. This time the convoys proved elusive. Meisel combed the area from north-west to south-east and back again, but not a single ship was sighted. In fact, he was too far to the south. So, on 20 December, Meisel decided to try his luck farther to the east, astride the sea lane between Britain and West Africa. He refuelled again two days later and resumed his elongated search pattern, this time along an east–west axis. On Christmas Eve, Tuesday 24 December, despite all their efforts, Meisel and his crew found they had little to celebrate. That, though, was about to change.

Early on Christmas morning, some 700 nautical miles west of Cape Finisterre, they came across Convoy WS-5A, a troop convoy bound for the Middle East by way of the Cape of Good Hope. The first contact had been made by radar during the night, and Meisel cautiously shadowed it, keeping to the west of it. The convoy of 20 troopships had left Britain on 19 December, and it was now heading due south, deployed in four rows and six columns. Unknown to Meisel, it was also extremely well protected. Its ocean escort consisted of the heavy cruiser *Berwick* and the light cruisers *Bonaventure* and *Dunedin*, while the aircraft carriers *Furious* and *Argus* were also in the centre of the convoy, transporting aircraft to West Africa, so they could be flown on to Egypt. The *Bonaventure* was on the starboard (western) side of the convoy, *Berwick* ahead of it, and *Dunedin* on the convoy's port beam. Six small corvettes were also stationed around the convoy, to provide protection against U-boats.

The Arado Ar 196 floatplane was fitted to all of the Kriegsmarine's Atlantic raiders. This two-seater aircraft had a range of up to 670 nautical miles and so acted as an extremely useful reconnaissance tool. Its drawback was that it had to be recovered from the sea, which ruled out the plane's use in rough weather.

By 0340hrs, the *Admiral Hipper* had reached a position a little ahead of the convoy, 4 nautical miles off its starboard beam. Detection had been made by radar, but with dawn approaching Meisel planned to use torpedoes to cause as much disruption as possible, and then attack at dawn with his main guns. The attack got off to a poor start. At 0353hrs Meisel launched six 53.3cm (21in.) G7a torpedoes, at a range of what was just over 7,000m. All of them missed and probably combed harmlessly through the rows of ships. For the British, it was a close-run thing. A hit or two on either a crowded troopship or an aircraft carrier would have been disastrous. Meisel then continued to shadow the convoy until dawn but lengthened the range to 5 nautical miles.

At 0808hrs, as dawn broke, lookouts on the *Admiral Hipper* spotted the *Berwick* off their port beam. Both ships were on roughly parallel courses. With the rising sun illuminating the British first, the German cruiser was harder to spot. Visibility was poor and the British cruiser was just at the edge of visibility. So, Meisel waited until the light improved slightly, and at 0839hrs he opened fire. His first ranging salvo fell short, as did the next two, but at 0842hrs the German gunners achieved a straddle, but scored no hits. *Berwick* had been completely taken by surprise – her guns were still trained fore and aft, but at 0842hrs she began returning the German ship's fire. The duel lasted for the best part of 33 minutes, with both ships flitting in and out of visibility, thanks to spray and smoke. On the starboard side of the convoy, 3 miles astern of the *Berwick*, the light cruiser *Bonaventure* briefly joined in the engagement but didn't manage to score any hits with her 6in. guns.

As soon as the *Admiral Hipper* opened fire, the convoy altered course to port, and started steaming away from the German ship. As it went, the *Admiral Hipper* briefly turned its guns on the troopships, before they finally disappeared from sight, hidden by a thickening smokescreen. Over the next few minutes, she scored hits on two British troopships, the *Empire*

The view forward from the foremast of the heavy cruiser *Admiral Hipper*. A rangefinder for her 20.3cm (8in.) guns can be seen in the foreground, on top of the forward fire control position, just behind her armoured bridge. Although cramped, these cruisers were extremely well designed.

Trooper and the *Arabistan*. Then, she switched her fire back to the *Berwick*. The action continued until 0956hrs. During the duel, *Berwick*'s 8in. guns failed to achieve any hits on the *Admiral Hipper*, despite later British claims. However, *Berwick* was hit four times by 20.3cm (8in.) shells in the exchange, causing minor damage amidships and knocking out 'A' turret, killing five of the turret's Royal Marine crew. At that point, the *Berwick*'s commander, Captain Guy Warren, decided to break off the action and turned away to the east, making smoke to cover his withdrawal. Kapitän Meisel was also in no mood to continue the attack. After all, he hadn't expected to encounter a ship as powerful as the *Berwick*. While the *Admiral Hipper* emerged unscathed from the duel, it could have ended very differently. Any serious damage could have meant she would never reach port.

So, Meisel broke off the battle too. The British later claimed that they had driven the German raider off, but in fact it was the Kriegsmarine's standing orders that prevented a renewal of the action and consequently spared the troop convoy. All he had achieved was inflicting some damage to the *Berwick* and damaging two of the transports. Meisel withdrew to the west before turning north later in the morning. At that point he decided to head for the safety of Brest. His starboard engine was still faulty, and so it made sense to repair the ship before venturing out again. Later that day, Meisel was given a last-minute Christmas present in the shape of an unescorted Indian steamer of 6,078 tons, the SS *Jumna*. She was sunk by the German cruiser's guns as she tried to evade capture. There were no survivors. After that, the *Admiral Hipper* headed west towards the French coast and reached Brest safely late on Friday, 27 December. Although her cruise hadn't been particularly successful, the *Jumna* being her only victim, at least she had reached Brest. Now she could use the French port to continue her raids the following year.

Kapitän Meisel's return

While repairs were begun on the *Admiral Hipper*'s engines, and the cruiser went through a small refit, plans were laid for a more coordinated approach to commerce raiding, which was scheduled to begin in early 1941. Raeder was keen to deploy his two battleships in the North Atlantic, and *Gneisenau* and *Scharnhorst* had already attempted a sortie in late December, leaving a day after the *Admiral Hipper* first arrived in Brest. It had been cancelled due to a combination of mechanical problems and atrocious weather. So, this venture was postponed until late January. This would roughly coincide with the return of the *Admiral Scheer* from the South Atlantic. If the *Admiral Hipper* was repaired in time, then this raised the possibility of having two battleships and two cruisers at large in the North Atlantic, all at the same time. It was the decisive operation Raeder had been yearning for since the war began.

In Brest, work on the *Admiral Hipper* was speeded up, but her propulsion system needed more repairs than anyone anticipated, and parts had to be manufactured and sent from Germany. Eventually, on 29 January, she was declared fully operational. Kapitän Meisel planned to take her to sea as soon as possible, but clear skies delayed his departure until Saturday, 1 February 1941. His orders were to keep away from major convoy routes and to avoid any repeat of his encounter with the *Berwick*. That meant heading west, beyond the shipping lanes between West Africa and the Western Approaches. This dramatically reduced his effectiveness. The reason lay in events farther north. Operation *Berlin* had begun, and at the moment the *Admiral Hipper* sailed, *Gneisenau* and *Scharnhorst* were in the Norwegian Sea, where their new fleet commander, Admiral Günther Lütjens, was preparing to break out into the North Atlantic by way of the Denmark Strait. Put simply, he didn't want Meisel's activities to draw out the Home Fleet.

After entering the Bay of Biscay, the *Admiral Hipper* curved around onto a westerly course and crossed these shipping lanes without incident on the night of 2–3 February. On 7 February the cruiser rendezvoused with a waiting tanker, stationed in the mid-Atlantic at 45° North, 30° West, roughly 1,400 nautical miles due west of Halifax. This spot was well south of the main Halifax to Britain convoy route. That same day, Lütjens and his two battleships were less than 800 miles away to the north and approaching this same major shipping lane. As Lütjens wanted to achieve surprise, he requested that the SKL order Kapitän Meisel to hold off beginning his cruise until the fleet commander in *Gneisenau* gave the order. So, Meisel and his men were ordered to wait near their refuelling spot until 10 February. In fact, the order to begin cruising came a day early, on Saturday 9 February. It seemed Lütjens had made his attack, and now needed Meisel to provide a diversion.

Meisel did this in style. He headed west, then south-west, until late on 11 February he was approaching the convoy route from Sierra Leone to Britain, some 380 miles to the east of the Azores. His first victim was the freighter *Iceland*, a straggler from Convoy HG-53. She was sunk without managing to send off a distress message. Her crew were taken off by the cruiser before she was sunk by guns and then a torpedo. Meanwhile, Meisel's *B-Dienst* team told him it was likely a convoy was

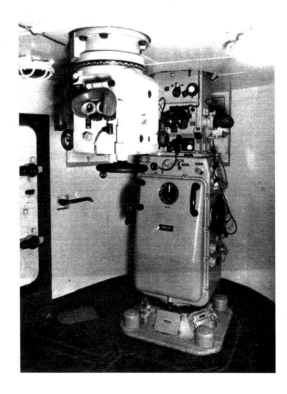

The after interior of the fire control position of a German battleship – in this case the *Bismarck*. The gun director dominated the compartment, while suspended in front of it is the periscope attached to the battleship's optical rangefinder. Similar equipment was fitted in the Scharnhorst and Deutschland classes.

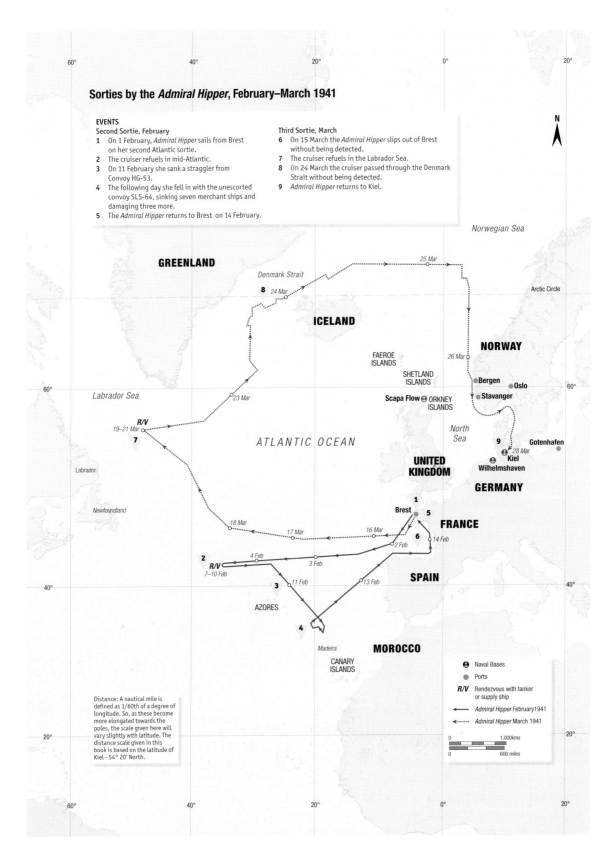

Sorties by the *Admiral Hipper*, February–March 1941

EVENTS

Second Sortie, February

1 On 1 February, *Admiral Hipper* sails from Brest on her second Atlantic sortie.
2 The cruiser refuels in mid-Atlantic.
3 On 11 February she sank a straggler from Convoy HG-53.
4 The following day she fell in with the unescorted convoy SLS-64, sinking seven merchant ships and damaging three more.
5 The *Admiral Hipper* returns to Brest on 14 February.

Third Sortie, March

6 On 15 March the *Admiral Hipper* slips out of Brest without being detected.
7 The cruiser refuels in the Labrador Sea.
8 On 24 March the cruiser passed through the Denmark Strait without being detected.
9 *Admiral Hipper* returns to Kiel.

N

Norwegian Sea

GREENLAND

Denmark Strait

25 Mar

8 24 Mar

Arctic Circle

ICELAND

NORWAY

FAEROE
ISLANDS

26 Mar

SHETLAND
ISLANDS

Bergen
Oslo

Labrador Sea

Scapa Flow
ORKNEY
ISLANDS

Stavanger

60°

23 Mar

*North
Sea*

60°

R/V
19–21 Mar

9
28 Mar
Gotenhafen

7

ATLANTIC OCEAN

Kiel

Labrador

UNITED
KINGDOM

Wilhelmshaven

GERMANY

Newfoundland

18 Mar

17 Mar

16 Mar

1
Brest **5**

2 Feb

6

FRANCE

2
R/V
7–10 Feb

4 Feb

3 Feb

14 Feb

40°

3 11 Feb

13 Feb

SPAIN

40°

AZORES

4

Madeira

MOROCCO

CANARY
ISLANDS

○✛ Naval Bases

● Ports

R/V Rendezvous with tanker
or supply ship

← *Admiral Hipper* February 1941

···· *Admiral Hipper* March 1941

Distance: A nautical mile is defined as 1/60th of a degree of longitude. So, as these become more elongated towards the poles, the scale given here will vary slightly with latitude. The distance scale given in this book is based on the latitude of Kiel – 54° 20' North.

0   1,000kms

0   600 miles

20°

20°

nearby, and sure enough, at dawn on Wednesday, 12 February, he came across his perfect target. It was homeward-bound Convoy SLS-64. In fact, Meisel had been looking for another convoy entirely, HG-53, sailing from Gibraltar to Liverpool. It had already been attacked by both U-boats and Luftwaffe bombers, however, and had lost six ships. The 18 undefended merchant ships of SLS-64 just happened to be in the wrong place.

It was arrayed in six columns and four rows and was steaming north at 6 knots when the German cruiser appeared from the west. Meisel attacked immediately, closing the range as the convoy scattered to the east, and firing at it with his ship's main and secondary guns. It was carnage. The attack began at 0605hrs, when the *Admiral Hipper* opened up on the freighter *Shrewsbury*. She was left wrecked, and the Germans finally finished her off with torpedoes. A few of the ships – *Derrydane* and the Norwegian freighter *Borgestadt* – tried to fight back using their single 4in. guns. Both ships were sunk, taking all their hands with them. Over the next hour, four more British merchant ships were sunk – the *Oswestry Grange*, *Perseus*, *Warlaby* and *Westbury* – and three more – *Ainderby*, *Clunepark* and *Lornaston* – were badly damaged. By then, the remaining merchant ships had scattered and were now out of sight, thanks to the poor visibility in the area.

By 0800hrs the attack was over, although a few of the ships like the *Westbury* were still sinking. Meisel left one of his potential victims unharmed. Instead, he ordered her captain to 'save the crews'. It was an impressive end to a very brief cruise. After the attack, Meisel decided to return to Brest. He turned away towards the north-west, and by dawn on Friday, 14 February, he was deep in the Bay of Biscay. He arrived safely in Brest that afternoon. By this stage, Lütjens' powerful force was still in the North Atlantic – at that moment it was refuelling to the south-west of Greenland's Cape Farewell. By then the decision had already been made that the *Admiral Hipper*, if at all possible, was to return to Germany for a thorough refit. Meisel reckoned

The heavy cruiser *Admiral Hipper*, pictured off Norway in April 1940. She was the first of the three heavy cruisers of her class to enter service, and to some extent was the most successful, both as a commerce raider and later as part of the Kriegsmarine's battle group stationed in Norwegian waters.

his cruiser would be ready to leave in a week. That would give him the chance to cruise with the two battleships and operate as part of a larger force. However, the usual engine repairs meant the cruiser wasn't ready to sail before mid-March.

The *Admiral Hipper* finally left Brest for the last time on Saturday, 15 March. She headed almost due west, and two days later she began crossing the Halifax to Britain convoy lane. She wasn't spotted, and sighted no ships herself. This was partly due to Lütjens, who had been operating against the same convoy route a few hundred miles to the west. So, that was where the British were concentrating their hunt, allowing the *Admiral Hipper* to transit this dangerous area without incident. The same was true of the *Admiral Scheer*. She was on her way home from the South Atlantic, and on 22 March she crossed the same convoy route a little to the west of the point chosen by Meisel. On 19 March, the *Admiral Scheer* refuelled from a tanker stationed to the south-west of Cape Farewell, and then began her run towards the Denmark Strait.

Again, bad weather helped screen her passage, and the transit was accomplished without incident on 23–24 March. The cruiser was now in the Arctic Sea, and Meisel made good time, heading west and then south, to pass through the Northern Passage on 26–27 March. The *Admiral Hipper* finally reached Kiel early on Friday, 28 March. Meanwhile, the *Admiral Scheer* followed an almost identical route, passing through the Denmark Strait three days after the *Admiral Hipper*, again without being spotted. She made it safely back to Kiel on Tuesday, 1 April. The brief sortie by the *Admiral Hipper* had yielded impressive results, and her safe return home was equally commendable. Raeder was delighted and welcomed both his cruisers home in Kiel. Their actions, it seems, vindicated his belief in the effectiveness of using powerful surface raiders in the North Atlantic. If he needed more proof, he only had to look at what his two battleships had achieved in the same waters.

Operation *Berlin*

On 14 October 1940, Raeder announced the Kriegsmarine would stand down from its commitment to support Operation *Seelöwe* – the invasion of Britain. So, after the rigours of the Norway campaign, he could finally earmark his most powerful ships for commerce raids into the North Atlantic. The trouble was, both *Gneisenau* and *Scharnhorst* were still in the hands of the dockyards, and then needed a period of crew training in

This schematic diagram of the Scharnhorst class shows how the armour was concentrated below decks, to protect the machinery spaces and magazines, as well as around the barbettes and turrets of the main guns. Despite British claims that these were 'battlecruisers', in terms of their armoured protection they were true battleships.

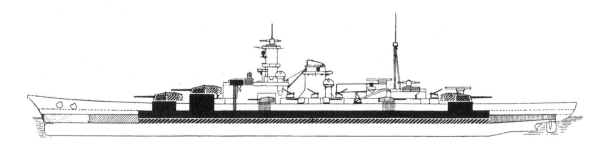

the Baltic. So, it wasn't until 28 December that the two ships could set out from Kiel. This sortie, codenamed Operation *Berlin*, involved an extended raid by both battleships in the North Atlantic. They were commanded by Admiral Lütjens, who flew his flag in *Gneisenau*. The timing couldn't have been worse. They were lashed by a hurricane-force storm off the Norwegian coast, and *Gneisenau* was damaged. On 30 December they put in to the Korsfjord near Bergen to ride the storm out, and to make temporary repairs to the *Gneisenau*.

Eventually the sortie was postponed, and the two battleships returned home through the Skagerrak. *Scharnhorst* went to Gotenhafen, while *Gneisenau* went straight into the yard in Kiel. The repairs were finished by mid-January, and Raeder ordered Lütjens to try again. Despite the false start, the whole operation was meticulously planned, with tankers and supply ships already sent into the North Atlantic, and supporting warships earmarked to help ease the battleships' passage through the Skagerrak, and on to the Norwegian Sea. They left Kiel at 0400hrs on Wednesday, 22 January, and by 0830hrs they had passed through the Great Belt, between the Danish islands of Fyn and Sjaelland. Then, they anchored while waiting for their minesweeper and anti-submarine escort the following morning. These escorts were delayed due to ice, and it wasn't until the morning of 25 January that they ventured into the Skagerrak. The rest of the voyage up the Norwegian coast passed without incident, and it seemed they hadn't been detected.

Dawn on 26 January brought clear skies, however, so rather than attempt the Faeroes gap, Lütjens decided to head into the Arctic Sea, refuel from the tanker *Adria*, and then try the Denmark Strait. A deterioration in visibility encouraged Lütjens to change his mind, and at midnight he ordered a course change towards the south-west, and the Faeroes gap. The force arrived there shortly before midnight the following evening and began the transit. At first, *Gneisenau* was in the lead, but when her radar broke down the flagship dropped behind *Scharnhorst*. Then, at 0620hrs on Tuesday, 28 January, a contact appeared on *Scharnhorst*'s radar. The target then became visible and appeared to be an enemy cruiser. Fearing this ship was part of a more powerful force, Lütjens gave the order to reverse course. Quietly the two battleships turned about and headed back towards the Artic Sea. The contact was actually the light cruiser *Naiad*, which had sighted the Germans too.

So, the British now knew that Lütjens was at sea. The new commander of the Home Fleet, Admiral John Tovey, already had the battlecruiser *Repulse* and four destroyers in the area, but other warships were soon sent north to reinforce this

The advantage of using capital ships as commerce raiders was that they could engage their targets from ranges of up to 20 nautical miles. This meant that only darkness or poor visibility could prevent them from demolishing a convoy. The shells pictured here are 38cm high-explosive ones – the kind carried by *Bismarck*.

THE ATTACK ON CONVOY HX-106

8 February 1941

During Operation *Berlin*, the German battleships *Gneisenau* and *Scharnhorst* broke out into the North Atlantic, with the intent of attacking Allied transatlantic convoys. Admiral Lütjens, who commanded the German battlegroup, began his hunt on 7 February, astride the convoy route from Canada to the United Kingdom. The following morning, while 700 nautical miles to the east of Halifax, the flagship *Gneisenau* sighted funnel smoke to the south-east. Earlier, *Gneisenau* and *Scharnhorst* had split up, to increase their chances of encountering a convoy. Now, he ordered both ships to angle towards the convoy, like two pincers, with *Gneisenau* to the north and *Scharnhorst* to the south. He estimated that by 1000hrs both ships would be within range of the convoy. Their prey was HX-106, a convoy of 41 merchant ships bound from Halifax to Liverpool. Unknown to Lütjens, though, as well as their usual escort of four destroyers, HX-106 was protected by the old Royal Sovereign-class battleship *Ramillies*. Just as both ships were almost in position, Kapitän Fein of the *Scharnhorst* spotted the British battleship and radioed the news to Lütjens. The German fleet commander immediately called off the attack and broke contact.

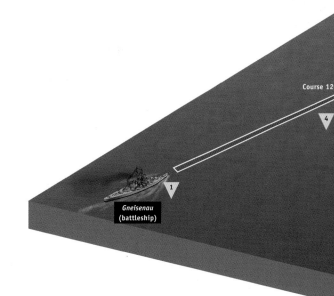

Gneisenau
(battleship)

Course 345°

Course 120°

▼ EVENTS

1. 0845: *Gneisenau* approaches estimated position of convoy on course of 120°, at 25 knots. The range to the convoy is approximately 43,000 yards.

2. 0845: *Scharnhorst* angles towards the convoy from the south, steering 060° and making 25 knots.

3. 0845: Unaware of the Germans' approach, Convoy HX-106 continues on its base course of 090°, making 8 knots.

4. 0912: Funnel smoke is sighted from bridge of *Gneisenau*. Lütjens confirms this is his target convoy.

5. 0947: At a range of 25,000 yards, *Scharnhorst* spots the masthead of an enemy battleship. Captain Hoffmann sends a wireless signal to the flagship, informing Lütjens of his sighting.

6. 0950: On board the *Ramillies*, smoke is spotted to the south. However, the battleship's commander Captain Read remains with the convoy, rather than altering course to investigate.

7. 0958: The decoded sighting report is shown to Lütjens on *Gneisenau*'s bridge. He immediately orders both German battleships to break off the attack.

8. 1000: *Scharnhorst* breaks contact and alters onto a new course of 180°, while increasing her speed to 28 knots. She is soon out of visual sighting range of *Ramillies*.

9. 1001: Similarly, *Gneisenau* turns away from the convoy and settles on a new course of 345° and a speed of 28 knots. Lütjens orders the *Scharnhorst* to rejoin the flagship at a pre-arranged rendezvous, 25 miles to the north-west.

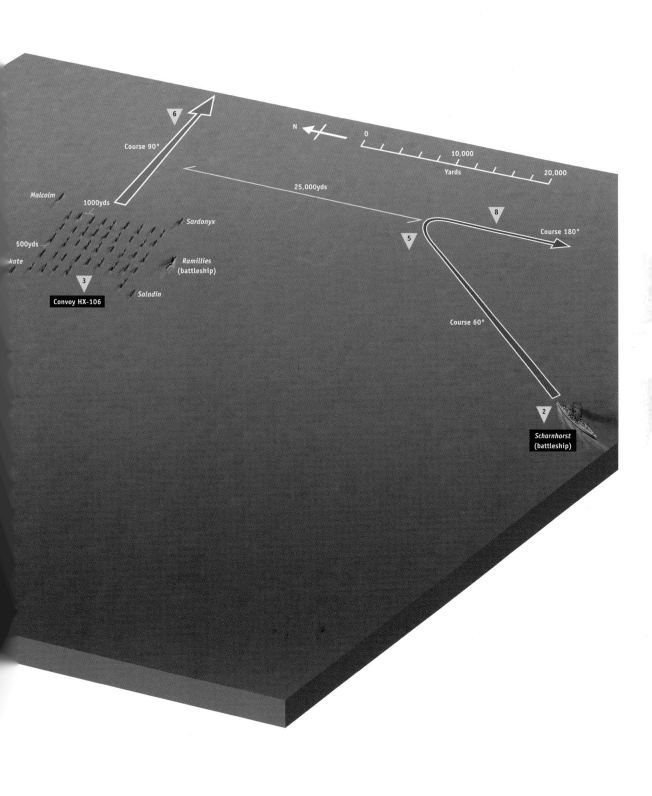

6

Course 90°

N

0   10,000
                    Yards   20,000

Malcolm

1000yds

Sardonyx

25,000yds

8

Course 180°

500yds

Ramillies
(battleship)

5

kate

3

Saladin

Course 60°

Convoy HX-106

2

Scharnhorst
(battleship)

Admiral Günther Lütjens (1889–1941), the fleet commander who commanded *Gneisenau* and *Scharnhorst* with such success during Operation *Berlin*. His success during this sortie meant he was ordered to repeat the sortie during Operation *Rheinübung*, flying his flag in the ill-fated *Bismarck*.

patrol and to guard the Denmark Strait. Lütjens had expected this, and headed north to the vicinity of Jan Mayen Island and the waiting *Adria* until the hue and cry died down. On 2 February he turned south again and began a cautious approach to the Denmark Strait, arriving there late in the evening of Friday, 3 February. By that time Tovey had sent the bulk of his ships away to refuel. Lütjens was lucky. Fog banks spread in from the Greenland side of the channel, and visibility dropped. At 0330hrs, *Gneisenau* detected a ship ahead of them on radar, so the fleet commander altered course to avoid her. They weren't spotted, and by dawn they were clear of the strait.

For Lütjens this was a triumphant moment. He celebrated by reaching for the flagship's tannoy, announcing to the crew, 'For the first time in history, German battleships have reached the Atlantic!' With that danger behind them, the battleships continued to the south-west, skirting the Greenland pack ice. On 5 February they rendezvoused with the waiting tanker *Schlettstadt* to the south of Cape Farewell. After refuelling, Lütjens led the two battleships towards the south-east. Intelligence reports suggested the homeward-bound convoy HX-106 was in the area, and the fleet commander had decided to attack it. At dawn on Saturday, 8 February, the German lookouts spotted smoke and then the masts of a convoy. It was HX-106, roughly 700 nautical miles to the east of Halifax. Lütjens had already decided to divide his forces, with *Scharnhorst* dispatched to attack it from the south, while *Gneisenau* moved in from the north-west.

This large convoy of 41 merchant ships was deployed in nine columns and five rows, spanning almost 4 miles of ocean. It was heading due east at 8 knots. Lütjens expected this convoy would be protected, but probably by nothing larger than a cruiser. By 0930hrs both the German ships were within the effective range of their 28cm (11in.) main guns. Then, at 0947hrs, the whole situation changed. Lookouts on *Scharnhorst*, to the south of the convoy, spotted the tripod foremast of a British battleship. The battleship's commander, Kapitän Kurt-Caesar Hoffmann, quickly passed the news on to the flagship, and at 0900hrs, when he received the signal, Lütjens ordered his ships to break contact. The foremast belonged to the venerable Royal Sovereign-class battleship *Ramillies*, armed with eight 15in. (38cm) guns. However, they weren't called upon to fire that morning, as although the British lookouts had spotted *Scharnhorst* to the south, the battleship stayed with the convoy.

Lütjens has been criticized for his excessive caution, but he was merely following the strict orders of Raeder. He was there to attack merchant ships, not engage in avoidable duels with enemy battleships. In fact, Hoffmann had tried and failed to draw the *Ramillies* away from the convoy, to allow the *Gneisenau* to attack it. However, the fleet commander's orders had ended Hoffmann's attempt before it had begun. The convoy then continued on its way, and reached Liverpool ten days later. *Ramillies* reported the sighting to the Admiralty but misidentified the German ship, naming her as the *Admiral Hipper*. So, the British remained blithely unaware that two German battleships were at large in the Atlantic.

Meanwhile, Lütjens withdrew to his supply area off Greenland, where both battleships refuelled from the tankers *Schlettstadt* and *Esso Hamburg*. Another problem was that *Gneisenau*'s engines had become contaminated by sea water, and she needed time to effect repairs. At that moment, the *Admiral Hipper* was at large far to the south-west, and so Lütjens hoped this would draw any other British capital ships away from him. On Sunday, 16 February, the battleships headed south again, but farther to the west than before. Word had reached Lütjens that another convoy had left Halifax, and he hoped to intercept it. Instead, on 17 February they sighted a lone merchant ship through the rain squalls, but Lütjens didn't attack, in case the larger convoy was nearby. The ship got away. Then, on 22 February, his luck changed.

Early that morning *Scharnhorst* detected a contact on radar, and at dawn smoke was seen to the west. Soon, several ships were sighted – all unescorted. Allied practice was to disperse westbound convoys 500 miles east of Newfoundland, so they could reach their destination ports independently. The two battleships swung into action and within minutes had sunk the first merchant steamer, the *Kantara*. Four more sinkings followed – the British freighters *A. Duff* and *Trelawney*, and the British tankers *Harlesden* and *Lustrous*. In all, these five ships displaced 25,784 tons. It was an impressive start to Operation *Berlin*. After the attack, Lütjens headed southwards, towards a new rendezvous point with a pair of support ships stationed in the Sargasso Sea. He reached the *Ermland* and *Breme* on Thursday, 27 February, and transferred the 187 prisoners taken during the attacks five days before. Then, with their fuel tanks replenished, the battleships continued on their way.

Now, Lütjens planned to head east, to attack the convoy route between West Africa and Britain. By 3 March he was to the west of the Canary Islands and astride the convoy routes. After another refuelling, the battleships began their hunt; this time, as the seas were calmer, they were able to fly off floatplanes to widen their search area. Contact was made with a U-boat, *U-124*, which, it transpired, was hunting for

Scharnhorst (pictured here) and her sister ship *Gneisenau* usually operated together, and first saw action in the Faeroes gap in November 1939, when they sank the armed merchant cruiser *Rawalpindi*. They subsequently operated together during the Norwegian campaign of 1940, and then again during Operation *Berlin*.

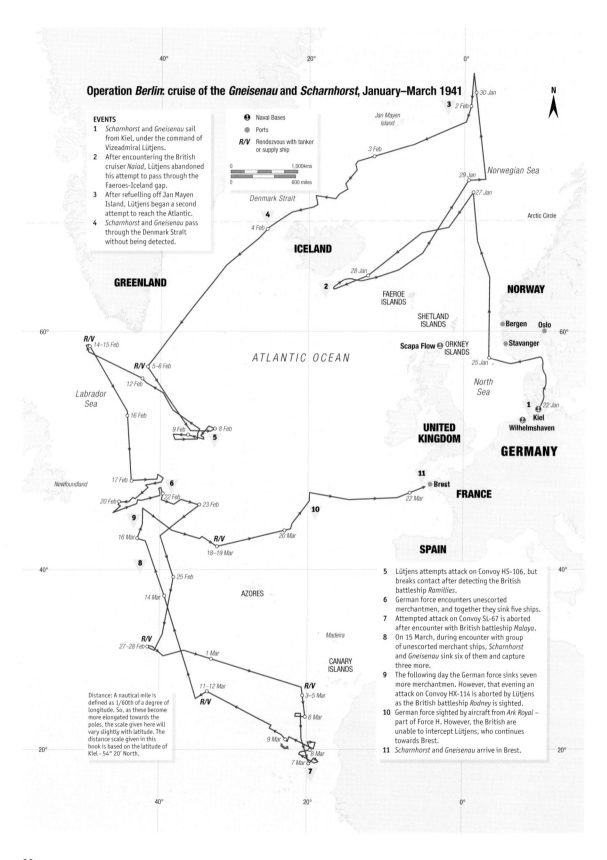

Operation *Berlin*: cruise of the *Gneisenau* and *Scharnhorst*, January–March 1941

EVENTS

1 *Scharnhorst* and *Gneisenau* sail from Kiel, under the command of Vizeadmiral Lütjens.
2 After encountering the British cruiser *Naiad*, Lütjens abandoned his attempt to pass through the Faeroes-Iceland gap.
3 After refuelling off Jan Mayen Island, Lütjens began a second attempt to reach the Atlantic.
4 *Scharnhorst* and *Gneisenau* pass through the Denmark Strait without being detected.

⊕ Naval Bases
● Ports
R/V Rendezvous with tanker or supply ship

0   1,000kms
0   600 miles

5 Lütjens attempts attack on Convoy HS-106, but breaks contact after detecting the British battleship *Ramillies*.
6 German force encounters unescorted merchantmen, and together they sink five ships.
7 Attempted attack on Convoy SL-67 is aborted after encounter with British battleship *Malaya*.
8 On 15 March, during encounter with group of unescorted merchant ships, *Scharnhorst* and *Gneisenau* sink six of them and capture three more.
9 The following day the German force sinks seven more merchantmen. However, that evening an attack on Convoy HX-114 is aborted by Lütjens as the British battleship *Rodney* is sighted.
10 German force sighted by aircraft from *Ark Royal* – part of Force H. However, the British are unable to intercept Lütjens, who continues towards Brest.
11 *Scharnhorst* and *Gneisenau* arrive in Brest.

Distance: A nautical mile is defined as 1/60th of a degree of longitude. So, as these become more elongated towards the poles, the scale given here will vary slightly with latitude. The distance scale given in this book is based on the latitude of Kiel - 54° 20' North.

two enemy battleships. Clearly another U-boat had spotted but failed to properly recognize *Gneisenau* and *Scharnhorst*. This hunt was called off, and the battleships continued on their way. Then, on 7 March, *B-Dienst* intercepts suggested a northbound convoy was approaching, SL-67. Lütjens planned to intercept it. By dawn the next day, they were almost astride its path, 350 miles to the north of the Cape Verde Islands, steering towards the south-west.

Gneisenau and *Scharnhorst* were 10 miles apart, to search as wide an area of sea as possible. Visibility that morning was good, and the sea was reasonably calm. However, it was the Germans who were spotted first. At 1030hrs they saw a Swordfish floatplane approaching – the kind carried by some British cruisers and capital ships. Unknown to Lütjens, Convoy SL-67's escort included the Queen Elizabeth-class battleship *Malaya*, as well as two destroyers. The Swordfish belonged to the *Malaya*. When her crew reported the sighting, *Malaya* and the two destroyers took up station 5 miles to the west of the convoy, to protect it from the approaching battleships. At around 1050hrs, lookouts on *Gneisenau* spotted the foremast of the *Malaya*, and Lütjens realized what he was facing. He immediately ordered both battleships to turn about and break contact. *Gneisenau* had also been spotted from *Malaya*, and from the destroyer *Forester*, but the British ships stayed with their convoy.

This was the second time in four weeks that Lütjens had turned away from a fight. Still, he was offered a small consolation prize. On Sunday, 9 March, *Scharnhorst* came upon the British freighter *Marathon*, of 7,296 tons, and sank her after taking her crew prisoner. After that, Lütjens headed to the north-east and a much-needed rendezvous with the tankers *Uckermark* and *Ermland*. They made contact on 11 March, and the refuelling was completed the following day. This time though, Lütjens planned to take the tankers with him, to double the area covered by his force's lookouts. Lütjens headed towards the north-north-west, until he reached the latitude of 40° 30' North – the latitude of New York. He then began a sweep northwards, hoping to come across more dispersed ships. He was in luck.

At dawn on Saturday, 15 March, his four ships were strung out in a line, with each ship 20,000m apart, at the limit of visibility. This allowed them

Scharnhorst sighted by the battleship *Malaya*'s floatplane, March 1941

On 7 March, at the height of Operation *Berlin*, Admiral Lütjens placed his two battleships *Gneisenau* and *Scharnhorst* astride the busy convoy route from West Africa to Britain. His *B-Dienst* intelligence-gathering section had discovered an Allied convoy, SL-67, was nearby, and Lütjens decided to attack it. He approached it during the night, and at dawn on 8 March his two ships were heading to intercept it, his battleships strung out 10 miles apart, so they could cover as much sea as possible. Then, at 1040hrs, German lookouts spotted a small British floatplane. Lütjens didn't know it, but the convoy escort had been reinforced by the Queen Elizabeth battleship *Malaya*. The Fairey Swordfish Mark I floatplane had been launched from the battleship just a few minutes earlier. After 'buzzing' the *Scharnhorst* at 2,500ft, this Swordfish flew on to inspect the admiral's flagship *Gneisenau*. It then kept a respectable distance from both ships, as it radioed reports of their actions to the battleship. Then, at 1050hrs, lookouts on *Gneisenau* spotted the foremast of the *Malaya* some 20 miles away off their starboard bow. In keeping with his strict orders to avoid fighting enemy ships of equal strength, Lütjens called off the attack and ordered his two battleships to turn around and break off contact. This plate shows the moment the Swordfish passed over the *Scharnhorst*. Although the battleship's flak guns were manned and ready, Captain Hoffmann decided not to open fire, for fear of alerting the convoy.

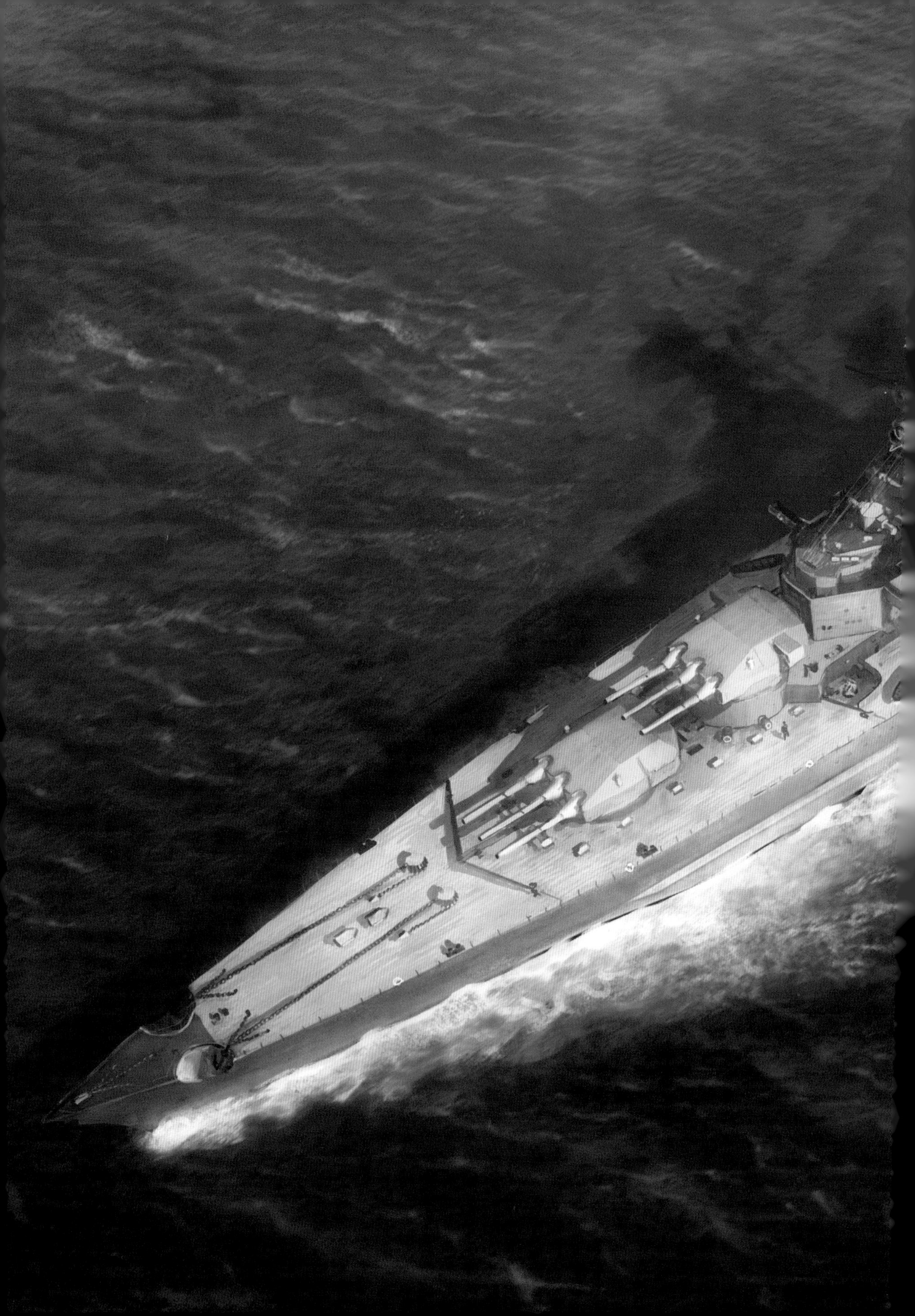

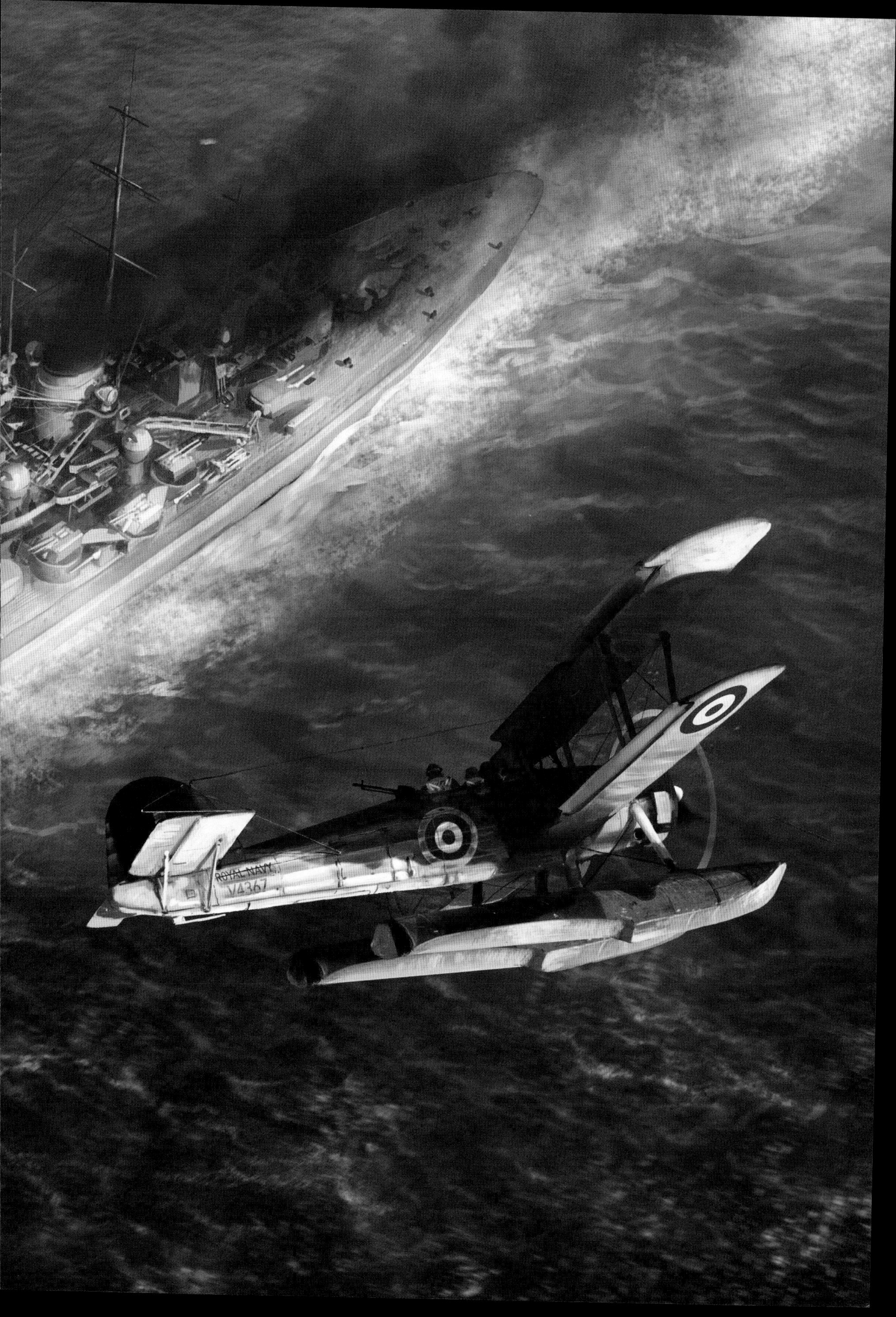
ROYAL NAVY
V4367

to cover almost 50 nautical miles of ocean. They were on a north-north-westerly course of 330° and making 12 knots. Then, lookouts on the tanker *Uckermark*, first in the search line, spotted what looked like two tankers ahead of them. She signalled the flagship *Gneisenau*, on her starboard beam, and the battleship surged forward to investigate. So began what turned out to be a very busy morning for Lütjens and his crews. The first victims were the British tankers *Simnia* and *San Cisimiro*. They were the ships spotted by the *Uckermark*. The *Gneisenau* sank the *Simnia*, and although three British sailors were killed, the remaining 57 men were taken prisoner. The *San Cisimiro* was captured intact and sent off to Germany with a prize crew – but not before she managed to send off a distress signal. This, though, was only the start of the morning's work.

Four hours later and 80 nautical miles farther to the north, they came across a cluster of one tanker and three cargo ships. One of them, the *Rio Dorado*, tried to run and was sunk by *Gneisenau* with all hands. The other three – the tanker *British Strength* and two cargo ships, the British *Royal Crown* and the French *Myson* – were all sunk after their crews were taken prisoner. Then, over to the west, trying desperately to escape, they came across three tankers – the British *Athelfoam* and the Norwegian *Bianca* and *Polykarp*. The *Athelfoam* was sunk, and the survivors of her crew were taken on board the *Scharnhorst*, while the *Bianca* was captured, and a prize crew sent aboard her. That day, the two battleships sank six ships and captured three more – in total just over 45,000 tons of Allied shipping. It turned out that these ships, encountered roughly 500 nautical miles from Newfoundland, had all just been dispersed from westbound convoys. Lütjens realized this meant other ships might be close by.

Darkness ended the hunt that day, but the following morning, Sunday, 16 March, the searchers were quickly rewarded with yet more victims. The first were the *Empire Industry*, a British cargo ship sunk by *Scharnhorst*, and then the Norwegian freighter *Granli*, which was sunk by the *Gneisenau*. Both had recently left outward-bound convoys. Farther to the north were the large Dutch cargo ship *Mangkai* and the smaller British one *Sardinian Prince*. Both were sunk, but the Dutch ship tried to escape and was shelled before her crew could abandon ship. Thirty-six crewmembers were killed, and the remaining nine were taken prisoner. Hardly had all prisoners been secured than the *Scharnhorst* came across the *Silver Fir*, which was sunk with one casualty, and the survivors taken aboard the battleship. Shortly before 1100hrs the *Scharnhorst* overpowered the British cargo ship *Demerton* and captured her crew. A little to the west, the *Gneisenau* came across the small British refrigerated cargo ship *Chilean Reefer*, which put up a brief fight. Nine of her crew were killed before she surrendered, and her crew abandoned what was now a blazing ship.

It had been an extremely successful morning for Lütjens. He'd added another seven ships to his tally, displacing a total of 28,375 tons. He fully expected the killing spree to continue. However, the smoke from the burning

Chilean Reefer was visible for miles. And worse news was to come. The flagship's *B-Dienst* team reported that at 2010hrs the British ship had sent off a distress signal – the British would know exactly where he was, and the smoke would act as a beacon. So, Lütjens gave orders for both ships to escape to the east as soon as they'd finished rounding up the *Chilean Reefer*'s boats. At that moment, *Gneisenau*'s radar picked up multiple contacts to the north-west, at a range of 20,000m (10.7 nautical miles). It was a convoy, HX-114, of 40 merchant ships, which had sailed from Halifax five days before. Minutes later, the battleship's lookouts spotted the masts of the merchant ships. Attacking a lightly defended convoy would round off the cruise perfectly.

At 2035hrs the lookouts spotted something else. It was the distinctive superstructure and foremast of a British Nelson-class battleship. In fact, it was the *Rodney*, which had joined the convoy the day before. With her nine 16in. guns she would be a powerful adversary – too powerful for Lütjens to risk fighting. The rescue of the British merchant seamen was abandoned after just three of them had been taken on board the German flagship. On Lütjens' orders the *Gneisenau* turned away to the south-east, towards *Scharnhorst*, which was 8 miles away, with the tankers. Before she could flee the scene, she was spotted by *Rodney*, who flashed her an interrogatory signal at 2037hrs. Lütjens replied she was the British light cruiser *Emerald*. With that the *Gneisenau* sped away and disappeared in the haze. *Rodney* slowly turned to investigate, but by then it was too late – *Gneisenau* had gone. Amazingly, nobody on board *Rodney* recognized the German battleship. Her true identity was only learned later that evening, when they picked up the remaining survivors from the *Chilean Reefer*.

That close encounter with a more powerful British battleship was a warning to Lütjens that he couldn't ignore. The British Home Fleet would be searching for him and would no doubt try to block his return home through the Denmark Strait. So, he headed east, stopping only to top up his fuel one more time on Tuesday, 18 March. Then the two German tankers were sent on their way. Also lagging some way behind the battleships were the two tankers captured on 15 March. Two days later, on Thursday, 20 March, Lütjens' battleships were less than 800 nautical miles from home – a day and a half's sailing. That morning, though, a Swordfish aircraft from the British aircraft carrier *Ark Royal* sighted the *Bianca*, one of the captured

With her nine 16in. guns in three triple turrets, the ageing battleship *Rodney* was more than a match for either *Gneisenau* or *Scharnhorst*, although she was handicapped by her poor turn of speed. Here she is shown in a later camouflage scheme. In mid-March 1941, she was painted grey overall, with lighter grey upperworks and a darker grey hull.

The mess deck of a German battleship. While rations in the Kriegsmarine were often described as monotonous, the men were usually well fed, and at sea, stores were frequently replenished from supply ships.

tankers, which her prize crew were planning to take into Bordeaux. The carrier was part of Force H, which was providing cover for convoys on the West Africa to Britain route. The battlecruiser *Renown*, flagship of Vice Admiral James Somerville, went to investigate, and came across both the *Bianca* and the *San Cisimiro*. The Germans scuttled both ships before they could be recaptured, although the *Bianca* had to be finished off by *Renown*.

Then, at 1730hrs, a Fairey Fulmar from *Ark Royal* sighted *Gneisenau* and *Scharnhorst*. They were 140 nautical miles to the north of *Renown*, so there was no chance of intercepting them before nightfall. Darkness also prevented the *Ark Royal* from launching an air strike of nine torpedo-armed Swordfish against the German ships. During the night, Lütjens headed north at high speed, then turned east, heading direct for Brest. At 1815hrs, when he heard the news, Somerville sent *Renown* and *Ark Royal* speeding north. *Ark Royal* sent up search aircraft at dawn on Friday, 21 March, but they found nothing apart from empty seas and thick fog. It wasn't until 2014hrs that a Lockheed Hudson of No. 220 Squadron RAF Coastal Command spotted the two German battleships. They were heading east at 21 knots, escorted by a pair of German torpedo boats. With Lütjens just 120 nautical miles from Brest, and darkness approaching, Somerville was unable to intervene. Instead, he headed back to Gibraltar.

So, protected by Luftwaffe fighters, *Gneisenau* and *Scharnhorst* finally reached Brest at 0845hrs on Saturday morning, 22 March. The two battleships were cheered to their moorings. The following day, Raeder would travel to the port, to personally congratulate Lütjens on the success of Operation *Berlin*. During the 18,000-mile voyage, the two battleships had conclusively proved Raeder's use of powerful surface raiders in the North Atlantic. For him, though, Operation *Berlin* was only the start. When they met, Raeder also took the opportunity to ask his fleet commander to lead another Atlantic sortie, this time sailing from the Baltic. This new venture, built on the success of Operation *Berlin*, was codenamed Operation *Rheinübung*. This time, Lütjens would fly his flag in the most powerful ship in the Kriegsmarine – the brand-new battleship *Bismarck*. Given such exciting prospects, neither admiral could have predicted that Operation *Berlin* would be the last of its kind. When Lütjens tried to repeat his success in *Bismarck*, the venture would end in disaster.

AFTERMATH

For one week, between 16 and 22 March 1941, the Kriegsmarine had three surface groups at large in the North Atlantic. Granted, the cruiser *Admiral Hipper* was making the run from Brest to Kiel, while the cruiser *Admiral Scheer* was following her on her way home from the South Atlantic. There was a brief moment, however, when Admiral Lütjens had entertained the notion of forming an even more powerful hunting group by adding the cruisers to his own force of two battleships. He also had six supply ships and tankers stationed at various points around the North Atlantic, two of which he'd temporarily used to augment his own force's search abilities. But it wasn't to be. The cruisers returned to Germany, and *Gneisenau* and *Scharnhorst* put in to Brest. This notion of creating a powerful commerce-raiding force didn't go away, though. Instead, both Raeder and his fleet commander hoped to create an even more potent force and set it loose in the Atlantic.

This scheme bore fruit in the planning of Operation *Rheinübung*. The centrepiece of this sortie would be the new battleship *Bismarck*, then undergoing post-sea-trial modifications in Hamburg. With her eight 38cm (15in.) guns, high speed and excellent armour, she would be a real boost to the Kriegsmarine's offensive power. Still, before she could be released for active operations, her crew needed to complete a period of training in the Baltic. It was hoped that when she sailed from there, ideally in April or early May, she might be accompanied by at least two cruisers. However, *Admiral Hipper* was undergoing a major refit, and both *Admiral Scheer* and *Lützow* were also undergoing repairs. That just left the *Admiral Hipper*'s new sister ship *Prinz Eugen*, which like *Bismarck* was 'working up' to operational efficiency in the Baltic.

Flying Officer Kenneth Campbell (1917–41), a Scottish-born Cambridge graduate, joined the RAF at the outbreak of the war and served as a pilot in No. 22 Squadron, Coastal Command. He won a posthumous Victoria Cross for his successful torpedo attack on the *Gneisenau* on 6 April 1941.

A contemporary newspaper artist's impression of the torpedoing in Brest harbour of the *Gneisenau*, 6 April 1941. There are inaccuracies – the torpedo launched from Flying Officer Campbell's Bristol Beaufort struck the battleship on her starboard side, beneath her quarterdeck. Moments later the torpedo bomber was shot down, and Campbell and his three-man crew were all killed.

Raeder hoped that a sortie by *Bismarck* and *Prinz Eugen* into the North Atlantic by way of the Faeroes gap or the Denmark Strait could be tied in with a second sortie by *Gneisenau* and *Scharnhorst* from Brest. Even if they remained separate, the two groups could divide British forces and control the pace and extent of their commerce-raiding operations. The result, inevitably, would be a major disruption to Britain's lifeline convoys. If threatened, the two groups could combine, giving the Kriegsmarine its most powerful fighting force of the war. In the early spring of 1941 these were still embryonic plans, but the SKL's operations team were busily putting meat on their bones. This though, would change dramatically.

The first setback came almost as soon as the two battleships arrived in Brest. During Operation *Berlin*, *Scharnhorst* had developed mechanical problems – a fault with her boiler tubes. These had to be replaced before she could return to sea, and so *Scharnhorst* was out of commission. The work on her boilers would continue until mid-July. The battleship was moved south to La Pallice – the port serving La Rochelle, where her presence was discovered by a British photo-reconnaissance plane. That night, 24 July, she was bombed by 15 Handley-Page Halifax heavy bombers. In the attack, she was hit by a stick of five bombs, and holed by two of them. She was fortunate that three of them failed to detonate. As a result, not only was she out of commission for Operation *Rheinübung*, but she would remain out of action until November.

As if news of the boiler problems wasn't enough, Raeder's plans were about to receive another major blow. On 28 March the photo-reconnaissance section of the RAF managed to confirm that *Gneisenau* and *Scharnhorst* were now in Brest. The Home Fleet reinforced patrols in the choke points around Iceland and the Faeroes in case the German battleships tried to return to Germany. Meanwhile, Tovey's main body as well as Somerville's Force H stationed themselves to the south of Ireland, astride the direct path between Brest and the North Atlantic. The RAF mounted a series of heavy raids on the French port. The first attack – a hundred-bomber raid on the night of 30–31 March – was ineffective, as was a second one during the night of 4–5 April. In this last raid, a near miss to *Gneisenau* while she lay in dry dock led the Germans to move her to a more secure berth.

On the evening of Sunday, 6 April, a hit-and-run attack by four Bristol Beauforts from 22 Squadron, RAF Coastal Command, tried to penetrate the port's defences, but only one of them reached the inner harbour where the *Gneisenau* now lay alongside the quay. Its pilot, Flying Officer Kenneth Campbell, came in low and released his 18in. torpedo at a range of 500 yards (457m). Seconds later, the small bomber was torn apart by anti-aircraft fire, and Campbell and his three crewmen were killed. Their torpedo ran true, and detonated against the stern of the *Gneisenau*, on her starboard side, just below the quarterdeck. This solitary torpedo effectively wrecked Raeder's grandiose plans. The battleship's propeller shafts were buckled, she took on 3,000 tons of water, and both her propulsive and electrical systems were damaged. It would take months to repair. So, a large-scale two-pronged breakout looked increasingly unlikely.

Five days later, on the night of 10–11 April, the *Gneisenau* was hit again, this time by four 500-pound armour-piercing bombs dropped during the third hundred-bomber raid in less than two weeks. Although two of the bombs failed to detonate, the others caused carnage among the battleship's exposed flak crews, killing 90 crewmen. A further 17 later died of their injuries. Thanks to these hits by bomb and torpedo, *Gneisenau* would remain in Brest's dry dock until the end of the year. In effect, Raeder had lost two of his three battleships, and the whole southern pincer of his large-scale Atlantic raid. Operation *Rheinübung* would go ahead, under Admiral Lütjens' command, but now his force would only consist of the battleship *Bismarck* and the heavy cruiser *Prinz Eugen*. Lütjens had actually advised a delay until *Scharnhorst*'s boilers could be repaired, but Raeder would brook no delay.

Operation *Rheinübung* got under way late on Sunday, 18 May, when *Prince Eugen* left Gotenhafen, followed a few hours later by *Bismarck*. Having joined forces off Rügen, the two warships and their escorts passed through the Great Belt and entered the Kattegat at 0600hrs on Tuesday, the 20th. Having passed through the Skagerrak, they skirted the Norwegian coast to reach the Kosfjord near Bergen by 0800hrs on

While Brest provided the Kriegsmarine with a useful port and repair facilities on the French Atlantic coast, it was also within easy range of air attack from British airfields. So, great efforts were made to camouflage and protect the German warships based there during 1941.

Wednesday, 21 May. That evening they left their escorts and resumed their journey north towards the Arctic Ocean. However, they had been spotted off Bergen, and so Admiral Tovey's Home Fleet put to sea. Lütjens opted for the Denmark Strait, and it was there at dawn on Saturday, 24 May, that the two German ships encountered the battlecruiser *Hood*, flying the flag of Vice Admiral Lancelot Holland, accompanied by the battleship *Prince of Wales*.

In what became known as the Battle of the Denmark Strait, *Hood* was blown up by a shell from *Bismarck*, and *Prince of Wales* damaged sufficiently to warrant her breaking off the action. It was a stunning victory for Lütjens, but although they had now reached the North Atlantic, he was forced to call off the raid. *Bismarck* had been damaged by shells from *Prince of Wales* and was haemorrhaging fuel. So, he decided to make for Brest. That evening he successfully evaded his British pursuers, and detached the *Prinz Eugen* to cruise independently. For 30 hours the British had no idea where *Bismarck* was. She was finally spotted by a British flying boat at 1030hrs on Monday, 26 May, but it seemed she was too far to the east for Tovey's battleships to catch her. Then, at 2100hrs, she was attacked by Swordfish torpedo bombers from *Ark Royal*. One of these 18in. torpedoes struck her stern, damaging a propeller shaft and jamming her rudder.

Bismarck was now little more than a stricken beast. After a night of harrying attacks by Allied destroyers, *Bismarck* was finally brought to battle by Tovey at 0845hrs on Tuesday, 27 May. Over the next 45 minutes the *Bismarck* was pounded by shells from the battleships *King George V* and *Rodney*. By 0930hrs her guns had been silenced, and her twisted decks were ablaze. At that point the order was given to scuttle the ship, a process hastened by the British cruiser *Dorsetshire*, which fired torpedoes into her hull. *Bismarck* sank at 1040hrs, taking most of her 2,200-strong crew with her, including Admiral Lütjens. There were only 114 survivors. When news of *Bismarck*'s loss reached Berlin, Hitler forbade any more surface commerce-raiding sorties; the sinking of *Bismarck* marked the end of Raeder's great Atlantic strategy. It was now deemed too much of a gamble.

A planned sortie by the *Admiral Scheer* and *Lützow* for July was cancelled, and the decision made to somehow bring *Scharnhorst* and *Gneisenau* back to Kiel, accompanied by the *Prinz Eugen*, which had reached Brest safely on 1 June. This venture, codenamed Operation *Cerberus*, was carried out successfully in February 1942, despite damage to both battleships. After that, the Kriegsmarine concentrated its remaining surface ships in Norwegian waters, to counter the new threat posed by the Arctic convoys. In the North Atlantic, the emphasis moved from surface commerce raiders to U-boats. The Kriegsmarine's rapidly expanded German U-boat arm was now fully committed to the cutting of Britain's sea lanes. Here, the Allies gradually developed the upper hand, and despite crippling losses in merchant ships the transatlantic convoys continued to get through. Never again would a German surface raider play its part in this Battle of the Atlantic.

ANALYSIS

With the benefit of hindsight, it should have been clear to Grossadmiral Raeder that his commerce-raiding strategy had limitations. The biggest of these was the size of the Atlantic itself. It stretched from pole to pole, and its 41 million square miles warranted its place as the second-largest body of water on earth. True, the Kriegsmarine's preferred hunting area of the North Atlantic was approximately half of this larger body, but it was still a lot of ocean for a raider to cover. Even when concentrating on the major shipping lanes between Canada and Britain, or Britain and West Africa, the expanse of sea a raider had to cover was immense. That, of course, made the spotting of convoys or solitary ships something of a lottery. Still, during the late 1930s and the early years of the war, Raeder and his staff found ways to improve the odds.

Admiral Forbes' successor as commander of the Home Fleet was Admiral Sir John Tovey (1885–1971). A skilled strategist, Tovey orchestrated the hunt for German Atlantic raiders during early 1941, a campaign that culminated in his pursuit and sinking of KMS *Bismarck*.

The development of accurate radio detection techniques – *B-Dienst* – gave the Kriegsmarine's raider captains a better chance of finding their quarry. Unfortunately for them, less attention had been given to the gathering of intelligence from other sources, such as U-boats or reconnaissance aircraft. Convoluted chains of command meant that it took time to pass on these sighting reports to the surface raider, a fact that also precluded direct coordination of U-boats, aircraft and surface raiders during an operation. If this problem had been properly addressed, and if the Luftwaffe had devoted more resources to marine reconnaissance, then these surface raiders might have been more successful. Of course, most commerce raiders had their own

The sinking of a freighter by a German surface raider operating in the Atlantic, 1939. Although this ship, the SS *Doric Star*, is unusual in that she was sunk by a torpedo fired from the *Graf Spee*, this scene was subsequently replayed dozens of times in the North Atlantic during 1940–41.

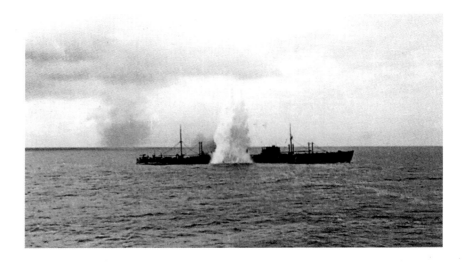

aircraft – one or more floatplanes. However, as these had to be recovered at sea, it made their use all but impossible during the bad weather, which often limited them to the southern portion of the North Atlantic.

Another problem with searching out the enemy was a simple mathematical one. A single ship had a finite search area, which in good weather might be as much as 20 nautical miles. Frequently, visibility in the North Atlantic was considerably worse than this. To improve the surface raider's chances, it made sense to operate in larger groups. For example, during Operation *Berlin* Lütjens used his two tankers to create a search line four ships wide. This quadrupled the size of his search area. All of these German raiders also carried radar, which gave them a better search capability at night or in bad weather. The trouble was, the range of German radars of this period was very limited, and the sets themselves were prone to breaking down. What Raeder didn't know was that the British had superior radar, and this technological edge would increase as the war went on. Still, with floatplanes, radar, good optical equipment and a *B-Dienst* unit, the commander of a German raider had a reasonably effective set of search tools at his disposal.

The other major German problem was reaching the North Atlantic in the first place. A raider captain might have three effective routes into the Atlantic, but the proximity to British airfields and Scapa Flow meant that the most practical of these were the Faeroes gap and the Denmark Strait. The safe transit of either of these choke points depended on two factors – weather and the effectiveness of any British patrols. This latter factor was something the German commander couldn't control. The SKL could, however, use its intelligence-gathering networks to build up a picture of the Home Fleet's movements, and so suggest when the patrol covering each choke point was especially weak. Then it was largely down to the command on the spot choosing his moment. Equally important was knowing the Home Fleet's main force of battleships weren't at sea, and able to challenge control of the choke point.

The weather was one of the best tools a raider captain had. Weather conditions played an important part in almost all of the Atlantic sorties described here. A German commander preferred poor visibility when passing through a choke point guarded by British patrols. Once in his hunting area, the commander preferred better weather – good visibility to maximize his search range, and calm seas to allow him to operate his floatplane, to extend his search range even farther. Then, when approaching his prey, poor visibility also allowed a raider to creep up on an Allied convoy without being spotted. As weather and its forecasting was so important, every German cruiser or battleship operating in the Atlantic carried its own meteorological team, whose advice was augmented by long-range meteorological reports sent out by the SKL. In the Atlantic, this knowledge was key to a raider commander's success.

In mid-1940, the fall of France and the conquest of Norway and Denmark dramatically changed the whole strategic picture. First, the Royal Navy's Northern Patrol was withdrawn from the Northern Passage and moved back to the four choke points leading direct into the North Atlantic. This put a much greater strain on the Home Fleet's resources. It also meant that any sortie by the Home Fleet into the Norwegian Sea placed it at risk of attack from the Luftwaffe, operating from Norwegian bases. This meant any interception of raiders by the fleet's larger warships had to take place at one of the choke points. Here, due to their range from Scapa Flow, and the need for ships to refuel and crews to rest, the Home Fleet's commander had to rely on good intelligence to forewarn him of a German sortie. For the British, this reliance on good intelligence was the key to success.

Fortunately for the Allies, the British successfully captured a German Enigma code encryption machine and deciphered their naval codes. While this didn't produce a complete intelligence picture, it usually gave the Admiralty some knowledge of German naval plans and ship movements. Then, the Allies' own radio direction finding equipment spanned the North Atlantic, and so could help pinpoint a radar if her commander was rash enough to break radio silence. Coastwatchers from the French or Norwegian resistance could sometimes provide useful information, but the most useful tool was a regular programme of photographic reconnaissance flights over ports like Wilhelmshaven, Kiel or Brest. Over the Atlantic, RAF Coastal Command was able to operate search patrols into the mid-Atlantic, but of course their effectiveness was limited due to the relatively small number of long-range search aircraft available, and the usual problems of spotting and visibility.

These, then, all helped or hindered the ability of a German raider to hunt out Allied merchant ships. Once the raiders encountered them, even if they formed part of a weakly protected convoy, then the German commander had the speed and firepower he needed to wreak havoc. This is exactly what happened when the *Admiral Scheer* intercepted Convoy HX-84, or the other raiders came upon dispersed or unescorted convoys. The problem for the raider commander was what happened when he encountered a better-protected convoy. The strict orders to avoid fighting unnecessarily were a well-meaning attempt to limit the risks inherent in naval combat. If any one of these raiders had been seriously damaged in an action, then its

The ultimate German Atlantic raider – the battleship *Bismarck*. With her eight 38cm (15in.) guns, she was considerably more powerful than *Gneisenau* or *Scharnhorst*, and so both Raeder and his fleet commander Lütjens had high hopes for her as a commerce raider.

chances of returning to a friendly port would be hugely reduced. So, when Kapitän Meisel of the *Admiral Hipper* engaged the *Berwick*, or Kapitän Hoffmann considered using the *Scharnhorst* to draw the *Ramillies* away from Convoy HX-106, he was breaking the SKL's excessively cautious rules of engagement.

The result, of course, was that this also limited the effectiveness of these commerce-raiding cruises. On two occasions, *Gneisenau* and *Scharnhorst* avoided pressing through the Faeroes gap when they encountered light enemy forces – the *Rawalpindi* in 1939 and the *Naiad* in 1941. In both cases the fleet commander felt it unwise to force his way through the choke point, as he suspected these ships were merely the outer screen of a larger and more potent British force. The 28cm guns of a Scharnhorst-class battleship would be able to engage lighter-armed enemy ships at well beyond the range where the German battleships would be exposed to danger. If their protagonist were a British battleship, all of which had slightly superior gun calibres and ranges, then it would be the German raider that would be exposed to danger first. Hitler had deemed these risks unacceptable, unless there was no alternative to a fight.

If a powerful German raider made it into the North Atlantic, then the Admiralty's solution of using capital ships as convoy escorts was simple and effective. A large part of the Royal Navy's battle fleet consisted of relatively slow capital ships. By attaching them to key convoys, the Admiralty sought to afford these convoys adequate protection against German surface raiders. They were unaware of just how restrictive Raeder's operational orders were. Effectively, though, they rendered these well-defended convoys immune to surface attack. So, during Operation *Berlin*, the mere sight of *Ramillies*, *Rodney* or *Malaya* was enough to force Admiral Lütjens to order his own battleships to break off the attack. Although *Scharnhorst* had successfully drawn *Ramillies* away from Convoy HX-106, then *Gneisenau* would have had 41 merchant ships at her mercy. By minimizing risk, these German orders also minimized the potential fruits of success.

CONCLUSION

In 1938, when the Kriegsmarine drew up plans for a potential war with Britain, it was promised that this war wouldn't begin for several more years. Instead, in September 1939 it found itself equipped with the wrong types of vessels. Given its need to fight a *guerre de course* ('war of the chase') and attack British merchant shipping, it would have been better placed if it had sunk its resources into U-boats rather than capital ships. Even more *Panzerschiffe* would have been beneficial, rather than a class of modern heavy cruisers which lacked the range to venture far into the Atlantic. Raeder, however, along with several of his senior admirals, had believed that 'the most effective weapon in ocean warfare is the battleship itself'. Raeder's Plan Z concentrated on building a powerful balance fleet, rather than giving the Kriegsmarine the best tools it could to fight a commerce-raiding campaign.

Then, after the loss of the *Graf Spee*, the German high command became overly cautious. Now, while it had the battleships – *Gneisenau*, *Scharnhorst* and with two more powerful Bismarck-class ships in the offing – it was too risk averse to use them effectively. It wasn't just battleships that had their wings clipped. On the day the cruiser *Admiral Hipper* reached Brest in December 1940, after her brief fight with the cruiser *Berwick*, Hitler demanded Raeder assure him that, in future, a raider would attack convoys but avoid engaging their escorts. This was a near impossibility, but Raeder assured the Führer that his ships would only take on an enemy escort if it were clearly less well armed. In effect, Hitler's lack of understanding of naval warfare and Raeder's willingness to acquiesce meant that, from that point on, the Kriegsmarine's raiders would be rendered virtually impotent by their own rules of engagement.

The Kriegsmarine's fleet admirals and raider captains now had to be excessively cautious in a type of warfare that often rewarded initiative and audacity. In this light, it is surprising that these Atlantic raids achieved so much. During their sorties, *Gneisenau*, *Scharnhorst*, *Admiral Scheer* and *Admiral Hipper* had sunk 48 Allied merchant ships, displacing almost 270,000 tons. Raeder saw this as a vindication of his belief in powerful surface commerce raiders. Instead, he should have drawn the conclusion that this wasn't enough. It was less than the tonnage the Kriegsmarine's U-boat arm was often sinking in a month from the summer of 1940 on. The cost of building an oceangoing U-boat compared to a modern battleship was miniscule – roughly 2 million Reichsmarks, as opposed to 145 million for a Scharnhorst-class battleship, 85 million for a Hipper-class cruiser, or 200 million for *Bismarck*.

Then there were the personnel – the complement of *Gneisenau* alone would have been enough to crew over 40 U-boats. The obvious inference is that the Kriegsmarine might have made better use of its limited resources if it had begun to plan for a *guerre de course* from 1930, when its first Deutschland-class commerce raiders were

A damaged merchantman, in a detail of a copy of a painting by Norman Wilkinson. It was a regular wartime scene – a battered merchant ship, trying to limp home. Several such ships were badly damaged by shells from commerce raiders during convoy attacks in the North Atlantic during 1940–41.

taking shape. While the prestigious launching of a pair of battleships in 1936 and again in 1939 may have transformed the shape of the Kriegsmarine, and added considerably to Germany's international prestige, it muddied the waters. Instead of a navy designed to attack enemy commerce, and to police its own waters, the Kriegsmarine was developing into what Raeder had wanted it to be all along – a powerful balanced navy. Essentially, the lack of a clear role for the Kriegsmarine, and the growing emphasis on big-gunned cruisers and battleships, meant that it risked having the wrong fleet for the task it would eventually face.

As a result, these high-value cruisers and battleships were used as surface raiders in the Atlantic, a role they'd never been designed to perform. The result was that policy of excessive caution, and the placing of the most powerful warships of the Kriegsmarine in danger, far from the safety of a friendly port. The risks were certainly real. The fate of the battleship *Bismarck*, on 29 May 1941, bore a grim testimony to that. Her loss also marked the shattering end of what, until then, had been Grossadmiral Raeder's great vision of using his surface fleet to bring Britain to her knees. While that campaign in the Atlantic was already reaching its brutal climax, the true 'Battle of the Atlantic' was one fought not by the mighty battleship but by the lowly U-boat.

Scharnhorst and *Gneisenau* carried their main battery of 28cm guns in three triple turrets, two forward and one aft. In theory these guns had a range of up to 40,000m, but effective range was usually considered 35,000m, or 19 sea miles.

FURTHER READING

Bekker, Cajus. *Hitler's Naval War*. London: Macdonald & Co., 1974.

Brown, David K. *Nelson to Vanguard: Warship Design and Development, 1922–1945*. London: Chatham Publishing, 2003.

Campbell, John. *Naval Weapons of World War Two*. London: Conway Maritime Press, 1985.

Friedman, Norman. *Naval Radar*. London: Harper Collins, 1981.

Friedman, Norman. *Naval Firepower: Battleship Guns and Gunnery in the Dreadnought Era*. Barnsley: Seaforth Publishing, 2013.

Gardiner, Robert (ed.). *Conway's All the World's Fighting Ships*. London: Conway Maritime Press, 1980.

Gardiner, Robert (ed.). *The Eclipse of the Big Gun: The Warship, 1906–45*, Conway's 'History of the Ship' Series. London: Conway Maritime Press, 1992.

Gröner, Erich. *German Warships, 1815–1945*, Vol. 1 *Major Surface Vessels*. London: Conway Maritime Press, 1983.

Heathcote, Tony. *The British Admirals of the Fleet 1734–1995*. Barnsley: Pen & Sword, 2002.

Hodges, Peter. *The Big Gun: Battleship Main Armament, 1860–1945*. London: Conway Maritime Press, 1981.

Jacobsen, Alf R. *Scharnhorst*. Stroud: Sutton Publishing, 2003.

Konstam, Angus. *Battleship Bismarck 1936–41, Owners' Workshop Manual*. Yeovil: Haynes Publishing, 2015.

Mallmann Showell, Jak P. *Hitler's Navy: A Reference Guide to the Kriegsmarine, 1939–45*. Barnsley: Seaforth Publishing, 2009.

Martienssen, Anthony. *Hitler and his Admirals*. New York: Dutton Publishing, 1949.

Parkes, Oscar. *British Battleships, 1860–1950: A History of Design, Construction and Armament*. London: Seeley Service & Co., 1966.

Roskill, Stephen W. *The War at Sea*, Vols. 1 & 3, 'History of the Second World War' Series. London: HM Stationery Office, 1954.

Vulliez, Albert and Mordal, Jacques. *Battleship Scharnhorst*. London: Hutchinson, 1958.

Whitley, M.J. *Battleships of World War Two*. London: Arms & Armour Press, 1998.

Zetterling, Niklas and Tamelander, Michael. *Bismarck*: *The Final Days of Germany's Greatest Battleship*. Newbury: Casemate Publishing, 2009.

INDEX

Page numbers in **bold** refer to illustrations and their captions.